SUCCEED IN

Office Practice

STUDENT BOOK

N6

Theresa Geen   Darryl Geen

OXFORD
UNIVERSITY PRESS
SOUTHERN AFRICA

Oxford University Press is a department of the University of Oxford.
It furthers the University's objective of excellence in research, scholarship,
and education by publishing worldwide. Oxford is a registered trade mark of
Oxford University Press in the UK and in certain other countries.

Published in South Africa by
Oxford University Press Southern Africa (Pty) Limited

Vasco Boulevard, Goodwood, N1 City, Cape Town, South Africa, 7460
P O Box 12119, N1 City, Cape Town, South Africa, 7463

Oxford Succeed in Office Practice N6 Student Book

ISBN 978 0 190750459

Fifth impression 2022

Acknowledgements
Publisher: Yolandi Farham
Project manager: Ingrid Brink
Editor: Louis Botes
Proofreader: Kim van Besouw
Indexer: Betsie Greyling
Designer: Gisela Strydom
Cover designer: Cindy Armstrong
DTP artist: Warren Brink
Typesetter: Aptara
Printed and bound by: CG Direct Print (Pty) Ltd.

The authors and publisher gratefully acknowledge permission to reproduce copyright material in this
book. Every effort has been made to trace copyright holders, but if any copyright infringements have
been made, the publisher would be grateful for information that would enable any omissions or
errors to be corrected in subsequent impressions.

CONTENTS

MODULE 4

THE ECONOMIC ENVIRONMENT

MODULE 5

HUMAN RESOURCES PROVISIONING

MODULE 6

HUMAN RESOURCES MAINTENANCE AND ADMINISTRATION

MODULE 7

SUPERVISION AND MOTIVATION

HOW TO USE THIS BOOK

Welcome to the Oxford Succeed series for TVET Colleges. *Succeed in Office Practice N6* provides you with everything you need to excel. This page will help you to understand how the book works.

Flow diagram maps what you will learn in each module.

Module is divided into units so information is manageable.

Learning objectives reflect the latest syllabus.

Key terms summarise key concepts and new subject terminology.

Relevant case studies and articles bring information to life.

Power break activities allows for discussion and revision.

Difficult and new subject terminology is explained where it is used, and in the Glossary.

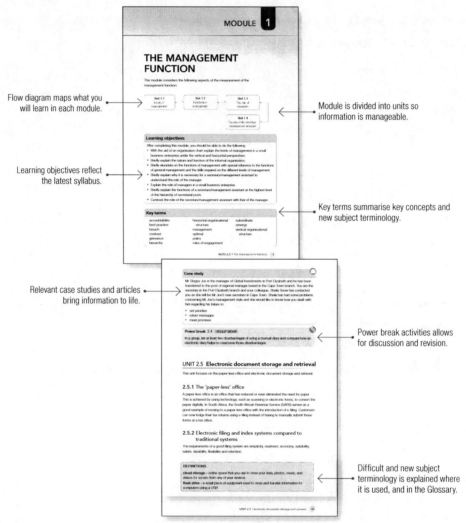

Other features:

? Did you know? boxes give interesting additional information.

Q Examples illustrate a point or provide practical worked examples.

- Diagrams, illustrations and photos provide information visually.
- At the end of every module, concise responses to the learning objectives are provided as a summary to use when studying.
- An Assessment section provides test and exam practice.

THE MANAGEMENT FUNCTION

This module considers the following aspects of the measurement of the management function:

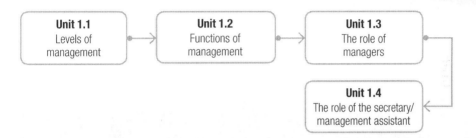

Unit 1.1
Levels of management

Unit 1.2
Functions of management

Unit 1.3
The role of managers

Unit 1.4
The role of the secretary/ management assistant

Learning objectives

After completing this module, you should be able to do the following:

- With the aid of an organisation chart explain the levels of management in a small business enterprise under the vertical and horizontal perspectives.
- Briefly explain the nature and function of the informal organisation.
- Briefly elucidate on the functions of management with special reference to the functions of general management and the skills required on the different levels of management.
- Briefly explain why it is necessary for a secretary/management assistant to understand the role of the manager.
- Explain the role of managers in a small business enterprise.
- Briefly explain the functions of a secretary/management assistant at the highest level of the hierarchy of secretarial posts.
- Contrast the role of the secretary/management assistant with that of the manager.

Key terms

accountability	horizontal organisational	subordinate
best practice	structure	synergy
breach	management	vertical organisational
contrast	optimal	structure
grievance	policy	
hierarchy	rules of engagement	

Starting point

Verushna has just started her first job at a big corporation. She is the personal assistant to one of the middle-managers of the organisation. As part of her orientation, the human resources department explained the organisational chart. This helped Verushna understand the different levels of management in the organisation and where her boss fits into the organisation. This information also helped her to communicate better with the different managers and to prioritise the different tasks she needed to perform for her boss.

Another aspect that Verushna found interesting is the different functions that the different levels of management have. She saw how her boss must plan, organise, activate and control the different teams and how the human resources department fits into management. Verushna now realises how her boss is involved formulating the organisation's vision, mission and policy and how these elements are implemented. She is also very impressed with how her boss deals with staff and shares the load in the team.

Verushna is sure that if she can learn from the managers she will herself one day become one.

Figure 1.1 Verushna is very excited to be learning more about management.

UNIT 1.1 **Levels of management**

Within all business enterprises there are different levels of **management** responsible for various aspects of managing the business enterprise. An organisation chart generally indicates how an organisation is managed. The organisational structures are generally organised in levels, either in a vertical or horizontal structure. This unit explores these structures.

1.1.1 Vertical organisational structure

A **vertical organisational structure** consists of top-, middle- and lower-management levels. The higher in the **hierarchy** the manager is, the more the authority and accountability that manager has. Conversely, the lower in the hierarchy the manager is, the lower the level of authority and accountability the manager has.

The organisational chart at Figure 1.2 shows the three levels of management in a vertical organisational structure. The chart shows the typical positions held within these three levels.

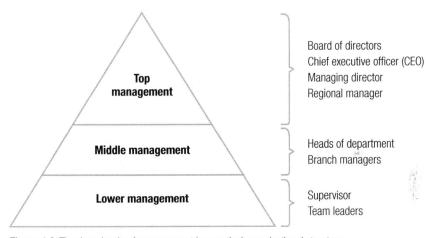

Figure 1.2 The three levels of management in a vertical organisational structure.

Information and orders are passed from the top levels down with very little communicated back up. Unit 1.3 covers the roles of the different types of managers at the various levels in greater detail.

> **DEFINITIONS**
>
> **management** – the people that collectively manage the running of a business enterprise
>
> **vertical organisational structure** – information and orders are passed from top management down to lower management
>
> **hierarchy** – the levels of authority in the organisation where the higher the position the greater the authority

1.1.2 Horizontal organisational structure

In a **horizontal organisational structure**, the business enterprise is organised based on the different branches or departments that management deem necessary to successful function as a business. Each department or branch has its own manager and all the department staff report to the manager. This organisation structure can be set up according to geographical regions, customer segments, functional departments, or even according to products.

Figure 1.3 gives an example of a horizontal organisation structure according to functional departments. The departmental manager has the authority and **accountability** and communication is quicker than in a vertical organisational structure.

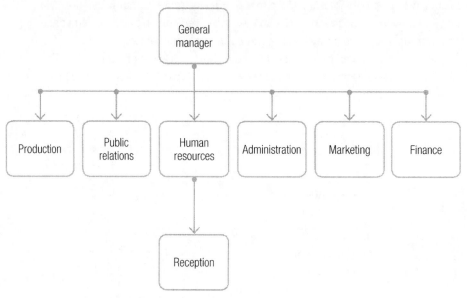

Figure 1.3 Horizontal organisation structure according to departments.

1.1.3 Nature and function of an informal organisation

An informal organisation is not governed by levels of authority or accountability but is based on social or cultural networking within the work environment. An informal organisation is the interlocking social structure of how the people within the organisation work together. An informal organisation can run at the same time as either the vertical or the horizontal organisational structure (formal organisation).

> **DEFINITIONS**
>
> **horizontal organisational structure** – flatter organisation structure where information and orders are from the senior to all employees reporting to him/her
>
> **accountability** – to take ownership of a task or activity whether it is completed successfully or unsuccessfully

Power break 1.1 INDIVIDUAL WORK

Study the diagram and answer the questions that follow.

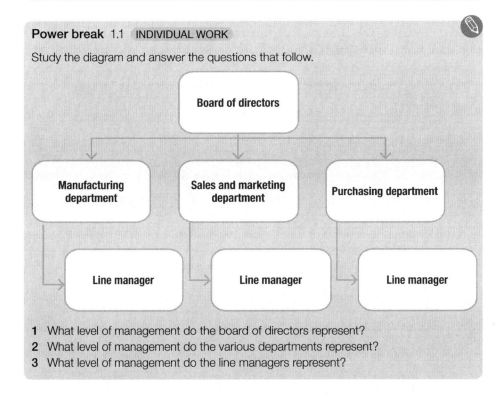

1 What level of management do the board of directors represent?
2 What level of management do the various departments represent?
3 What level of management do the line managers represent?

UNIT 1.2 **Functions of management**

In this unit we will cover the main functions performed by the general management of the organisation.

1.2.1 Functions of general management

As shown in Figure 1.4, the functions of general management are divided into five areas.

Figure 1.4 The five functions of general management.

We now consider each of these five functions in turn.

Planning

Planning covers long-term, medium-term, and short-term planning in the organisation.

- Long-term planning focuses on where the organisation would like to be in five to ten years' time. This is also known as strategic planning.
- Medium-term planning deals with where the organisation wants to be in one to five years' time.
- Short-term planning envisages where the organisation wants to be in less than a year's time.

Management planning activities include:

- setting workers' objectives/targets for the year
- formulating, understanding, and explaining the organisation's policies and procedures to all employees
- keeping up-to-date with new developments in the marketplace
- doing research and development on new products or services that will give the organisation a competitive edge
- improving work methods.

Organising

The organising activities of general management revolve around ensuring the capital (money), resources (machinery and equipment), labour and entrepreneur (management) are in place to complete a specific set of activities, such as making a product or rendering a service. These activities include:

- delegating work to an individual or team
- identifying which roles belong to which jobs (job specification)
- assigning activities to each role
- setting the **rules of engagement** for the team
- encouraging individual participation in group activities
- identifying employees' strengths and making sure that the team is balanced and able to meet its objectives.

> **Did you know?** Capital, natural resources, labour and equipment are referred to as the four factors of production.

> **DEFINITION**
>
> **rules of engagement** – written guidelines by which all team members are expected to behave, communicate, engage, support, treat, and coordinate with one another

Activating/leading

Leadership is defined as the ability to influence others. In this activity, general management are concerned about making sure that they influence others to reach a goal or objective. It involves the manager facilitating the procedures for specific activities by either showing the employees what needs to be done or explaining the steps to complete the activity. Leadership is also concerned with assessing each person's work and giving honest feedback. A leader provides coaching to employees to make them better workers who can be used in higher positions in the organisation. A good leader will share in the success of the team or employees and celebrate the little wins to encourage **subordinates**.

Figure 1.5 A manager using a laptop to discuss information with a secretary.

Controlling

Management must ensure that capital, labour and resources work together in a controlled manner to ensure that the enterprise's goals or objectives are reached. The controlling function includes:
- ensuring that the work and product is of a high standard
- making sure that all processes and procedures are cost effective
- controlling the accuracy and quantity of work delivered

DEFINITION

subordinate – a person under the authority or control of another within an organisation

---

- showing **best practice** in completing certain activities and sharing this with other employees that perform the same activities
- recording key learnings from day-to-day activities and taking corrective actions as needed.

Human resources/staffing

Human resources (HR) or staffing is a key function of general management. This function ensures that the organisation has the right people in the right positions and includes:

- formulating employee terms and conditions
- selecting the proper recruitment source
- initiating advertising of vacant posts
- screening candidates who applied for the vacant posts
- conducting interviews with short-listed candidates
- making an offer of employment to the successful candidate
- structuring wages and salaries of employees
- meeting all legal requirements for employees, for example, the Unemployment Insurance Fund (UIF) and the Basic Conditions of Employment Act (BCEA)
- undertaking induction of new employees
- setting goals and objectives for employees
- monitoring progress against targets that were set
- coaching/mentoring staff to perform at their **optimal** level
- addressing staff issues
- dealing with **grievances** and taking disciplinary actions.

The time that management spends on the different management functions is different at the various management levels.

- Top-level management provide the strategic leadership in the organisation and requires them to focus more on planning and co-ordination functions.
- Middle-level management provide management of a specific business activity like finance, marketing, or purchasing. They will spend most of their time on activating/ leading and controlling management functions.
- Lower-level management are responsible for supervising the operational staff. This requires them to focus their time and effort on activating, controlling, and human resource functions.

DEFINITIONS

best practice – the most effective and practical method or technique to achieve an objective while making the optimum use of the enterprise's resources

optimal – the level at which a person performs at their best or most effectively

grievance – an unfair or unjust action that may cause a person or group to lay a complaint against another person or group

---

1.2.2 The skills of a manager

A manager performs many tasks and functions in an enterprise and needs many different skills to perform those functions.

Figure 1.6 A manager performs many functions in an enterprise and needs specific skills.

These managerial skills can be divided into three main categories: technical, human, and conceptual. To complete some managerial tasks or activities needs a combination of all three skills categories. Figure 1.7 illustrates this interaction.

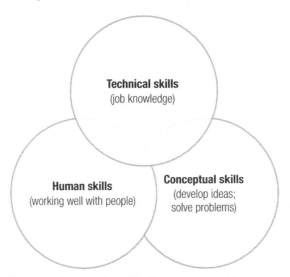

Technical skills
(job knowledge)

Human skills
(working well with people)

Conceptual skills
(develop ideas;
solve problems)

Figure 1.7 A combination of the three managerial skills.

Technical skills

Managers need to have the knowledge or understanding of a product, process, or service to be able to explain to non-managerial employees what they need to do and what standard is expected of them. For example, a production manager must understand the production process and the final specification of the product to explain it to anyone that needs to do work in that process.

Human skills

Managers must be able to manage the people who work for them in the organisation and must be able to deal with other stakeholders outside the organisation, such as government, suppliers, and unions. These skills include the ability to communicate effectively with others and understanding and motivating employees.

Conceptual skills

Managers should be able to understand abstract ideas and visualise the entire business – where it is currently and where it is going. They must think creatively and be able to troubleshoot complex problems.

Power break 1.2   INDIVIDUAL WORK

Connect the function of management in Column A with the description in Column B.

Column A	Column B
1. Planning	A. Delegating duties to subordinates
2. Organising	B. Setting goals, gathering records and improving performance
3. Activating/leading	C. Looking at opportunities and problems
4. Controlling	D. Structuring wages and salaries
5. Human resources/staffing	E. Explaining and checking tasks of subordinates

UNIT 1.3 The role of managers

The manager has a wide range of roles that need to be fulfilled to make the organisation a success. In this unit we will cover these roles in greater detail.

1.3.1 Roles of a manager

To understand the roles of a manager, we need to understand their impact on the following:
* formulating the vision, mission and **policy**
* implementing organisation and methods

DEFINITION

policy – a course or principle of action adopted or proposed by an organisation or individual

- decision making
- delegating
- dealing with staff.

We also need to know the manager's environmental responsibilities and the management capabilities required in the assigned management role/s.

Figure 1.8 The different roles of a manager mesh and combine to help keep the organisation moving forward.

We now consider the different managerial roles.

Formulating the vision, mission, and policy of the organisation

Planning is a key part of duties of the manager and here the manager will put in place the vision, mission and policies needed for the organisation.

The vision
The vision of the organisation is an indication to all stakeholders of what the organisation wants to achieve. Someone once said that a vision is a dream that is not fulfilled in your lifetime.

A vision for an up-and-coming airline company could be:

'To become South Africa's safest, most desirable, most flown and most profitable airline company.'

The mission

The mission of the organisation is how the organisation goes about reaching the vision that has been set in place. Here is an example of a mission statement from PEP Stores:

Figure 1.9 The PEP Stores mission statement

Policies/code of conduct

The policies of an organisation help to identify the standards of the organisation and provides guidelines for all stakeholders.

Implementing organisation and methods

Management is responsible for setting up the correct organisational structure that can deliver the goals and objectives of the organisation. This involves finding the balance of the number of departments, right personnel, right leaders, and right resources at each level of the organisation, as well as staying within the organisation's budget.

Management should define the methods the organisation will put in place that are most effective in giving the correct products and/or services required by the organisation's customers at the right place, the right price, and at the right time.

Decision making

For the organisation to reach its goals and objectives, managers must use the vision, mission and policies to make effective decisions regarding:

- systems and processes
- equipment and machinery
- resources required.

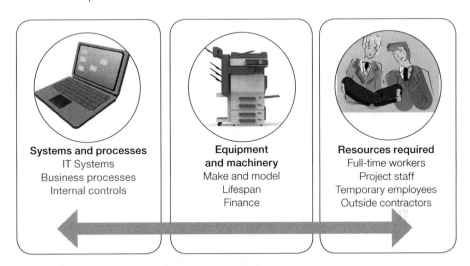

Systems and processes
IT Systems
Business processes
Internal controls

Equipment and machinery
Make and model
Lifespan
Finance

Resources required
Full-time workers
Project staff
Temporary employees
Outside contractors

Figure 1.10 Managers must use the vision, mission, and policies to make effective decisions about numerous aspects of the business.

Delegation

As we previously mentioned, leadership is the ability to influence others to do activities that are needed to meet the organisation's goals and objectives. Delegation is when the manager delegates (gives) responsibility to a lower-level manager or a non-managerial employee to complete a specific job, task or activity.

Staff matters

Key responsibilities of all managers include the hiring, leading, motivating, evaluation, and firing of staff.

Environmental responsibilities

All managers are expected to be environmentally aware and responsible. There could be financial and/or legal consequences if the manager does not comply. For example, if a manager allows the production department to dump waste products in an area where it could pollute a river or a dam, the manager could be held legally responsible for this irresponsible behaviour.

Figure 1.11 All managers are expected to be environmentally aware and responsible.

1.3.2 Characteristics of a good manager

A good manager should:

- work well in a team
- work well with others
- communicate effectively
- be a good listener
- remain calm, especially in a crisis
- adapt to change and be a champion for change
- provide employees with honest feedback
- admit mistakes and learn from them
- be able to negotiate and close sales deals
- solve problems and make effective decisions
- be confident and energetic
- have respect for all people
- effectively run meetings
- have good values and morals
- display integrity and honesty in all interactions
- be ethical in their business dealings
- confidently deal with crisis situations

Figure 1.12 A manager must work well with others in a team.

- be socially and environmentally aware and responsible
- have a solid understanding of basic finance (income statement, balance sheet, cash flow statement, etc.)
- be able to manage the administrative tasks of a manager
- be computer literate.

1.3.3 Why should the secretary know the role of the manager?

To do the job effectively, secretaries should know the role/s of the managers they work with. This will enable secretaries to help the managers in fulfilling those managerial roles. The manager and the secretary are a team and the secretary must prioritise work activities based on what the manager expects to carry out.

Power break 1.3 INDIVIDUAL WORK

Read the following passage and answer the questions that follow.

Management success

The success of any organisation depends on the main contributor, the manager. If the manager is successful in reaching the organisation's goals it means that the manager performed in his/her specific function. It is also important that the secretary understands the functions of the manager. The secretary will work in close cooperation with the manager in completing the manager's duties. It requires the secretary and the manager to establish a positive working relationship.

1 In your opinion, why is it important for any institution to be led by a manager?
2 How will close co-operation between the secretary and the manager benefit the organisation?
3 If you were the manager of the organisation list five key responsibilities you would focus on and why?

UNIT 1.4 The role of the secretary/management assistant

The primary task of a secretary is to support the manager or managers in an organisation. As shown in Figure 1.13, at the highest (fourth) level in the secretarial career the key positions for secretaries are:

- personal assistant
- executive assistant
- executive secretary.

This unit focuses on the role and functions of the secretary/management assistant at the highest level in the hierarchy of secretarial posts.

Level 4
Personal assistant
Executive assistant
Executive secretary

Level 3
Secretary
Senior secretary
Senior administrative assistant

Level 2
Junior secretary
Office assistant
Girl Friday

Entry level
Typist
Receptionist
Switchboard operator

Figure 1.13 The promotion route of a secretary

1.4.1 Functions of the secretary

The functions of the secretary can be divided into the following categories:
- liaison
- communication
- correspondence
- confidentiality
- reporting
- controls
- general tasks.

Figure 1.14 Secretaries and management assistants have several different functions.

1.4.2 Secretarial tasks

The following table lists the various functions of a secretary and some of the related tasks.

Table 1.1 The secretarial functions and some of the related tasks

Function	Related tasks
Liaison	Liaison includes: • answering telephone calls and liaising with clients • delegating work in the manager's absence • doing receptionist duties and dealing with visitors.

continued on next page ...

Function	Related tasks
Communication	Communication includes: • taking dictation for staff bulletins • preparing press releases on behalf of the manager • doing switchboard duties.
Correspondence	Correspondence includes: • reading, monitoring and responding to the manager's mail and email • preliminary drafting of correspondence on the manager's behalf • taking dictation of letters to customers, suppliers or other key stakeholders • typing documents.
Confidentiality	The word 'secretary' means 'secret' in Latin and all secretaries must, as a rule, not talk about confidential information outside of the organisation. • Confidentiality **breaches** can lead to losses for the organisation and a breakdown of the trust that the manager has in the secretary. • Confidential information should always be protected and should be locked away or be password protected. A secretary will deal with confidential information on a regular basis. This includes: • managing the manager's diary • dealing with confidential documents • preparing papers for meetings • performing subordinate human resource activities, such as performance evaluations, goal setting and coaching.
Reporting	Reporting includes: • conducting research • preparing presentations • typing documents.
Controls	Controlling includes: • recording action points and writing minutes of meetings • managing the petty cash system • training new employees on the administration requirements, for example, claiming for business expenses.
General tasks	General tasks include: • managing and reviewing filing and office systems • sourcing and ordering stationery and office equipment • organising complex travel • managing ad hoc projects • copying documents • undertaking mail room services • dealing with messengers.

Flashback to N4: You were introduced to the role of the secretary in Module 1 of *Office Practice N4*. Go back to your N4 notes and revise what you learned there.

DEFINITION

breach – to break a law or rule

1.4.3 Personal characteristics of the secretary

The successful secretary/management assistant will have certain characteristics.
The person will be:

- efficient
- discreet
- flexible
- enthusiastic
- cheerful

- loyal
- respectful
- self-motivated
- organised
- attentive to detail

- pro-active
- responsible
- a good communicator.

Power break 1.4 **GROUP WORK**

Verushna was appointed in her new job after successfully replying to the following job advertisement. Study the advertisement and answer the questions that follow.

Personal assistant/secretary

Provide administrative support to the company MARKETING MANAGER and ensure that all secretarial/administrative/support requirements are met. Support the marketing manager in the performance of all related duties and responsibilities in an organised and timely fashion, consistent with the requirements of the marketing manager's role, and in line with the operating practices of the business.

Academic qualifications
Grade 12 certificate or equivalent NQF level 4 Certificate
Diploma in office management/administration or Secretarial Diploma/Certificate/Computer Literate

Personal qualities required
The successful applicant will possess the following personal characteristics:
- excellent linguistic and written skills
- fluency in English and Afrikaans
- Internet and PC proficiency with MS Word, Excel and Outlook skills
- demonstrated experience with MS Word, MS Excel, MS Outlook and related programs
- experience with diary and travel management

- experience with conference calling facilities and internal telephone transfers
- effective communication skills, including the ability to effectively communicate requests and instructions to individuals and groups
- commitment to, and enthusiasm for, client service and delivery
- be self-motivated, flexible and adaptable in managing changing work requirements and varying volumes of work
- be attentive to detail
- demonstrate loyalty to the company
- ability to be discreet and confidential regarding all internal company matters
- ability to be proactive and to work co-operatively and effectively within the team and the organisation
- ability to manage multiple tasks simultaneously, solve problems, manage and meet deadlines, and maintain a high quality of work.

In addition, the successful applicant will possess a positive, cheerful and enthusiastic personal presentation that reflects a professional image and the values of the organisation.

---

1. Which of the qualities mentioned in the advertisement do you possess?
2. Which of the qualities in the advertisement are listed in the previous section: 'Personal characteristics of the secretary'?

1.4.4 Manager's expectations

As previously indicated, the manager and the secretary form a team and managers will expect their secretaries to fully understand what their (the manager's) roles and responsibilities entail. Managers expect secretaries to be able to prioritise their secretarial tasks according to the key deliverables of the manager. For example, if the manager has an important meeting with the shareholders, the secretary should pro-actively do all the necessary research, presentations and reports requested by the manager to effectively communicate with the shareholders.

In a situation where the secretary/management assistant supports more than one manager, the secretary/management assistant must establish a balanced approach in dealing with all managers. The managers and the secretary/management assistant must agree on how the work relationship will be managed, especially how the their time should be allocated between the managers. The secretary/management should meet with each manager regularly to discuss new work and progress on existing work. If there is an urgent request from one of the managers, the secretary should inform the other manager/s that the urgent request is being attended to and agree to continue with other activities once the crisis is resolved.

Figure 1.15 A manager and a secretary in a meeting

1.4.5 Contrasting roles of the secretary and the manager

The role of the secretary is divided into the following areas:
* assisting the manager
* assisting customers
* assisting other secretaries and work colleagues.

The secretary must fully understand the manager's role in the organisation as well as the manager's goals and objectives for the current year. This will make it easier to help the manager to be more efficient and effective in the execution of the job.

The manager, on the other hand, must support the secretary to ensure that the secretary is successful in the performance of the numerous day-to-day tasks.

The following table **contrasts** the roles of the secretary and manager.

Table 1.2 The contrasting roles of a secretary and manager

Secretary	Manager
A secretary should: • make the manager the top priority in the job • screen the manager's calls and visitors and deal with unimportant issues, delegating to others if necessary, and only give the manager high priority calls and visitors to attend to • maintain a high work standard to avoid double work, especially in preparing documents, reports or presentations for the manager • communicate with the manager regularly to ensure that the manager is kept up-to-date on all work requested. This communication is especially important first thing in the morning and before important meetings or appointments • remember the manager's likes and dislikes, for example, if the manager prefers an aisle seat on the plane, advise the travel agent of the manager's preference or make the bookings accordingly • be your manager's memory and give the manager timely reminders of important appointments • be professional and always deal with the manager with courtesy and respect • take responsibility for any mistakes you have made, by advising the manager of the error and make sure to correct the mistake swiftly • be a calming influence on the manager, especially in a crisis.	A manager should: • communicate clearly what is expected from the secretary • provide the secretary with the necessary access to the management diary and telephone calls • provide leadership and guidance when the secretary needs to prioritise different tasks • maintain a cool head and deal with the secretary professionally • spend time with the secretary to discuss upcoming meetings and appointments, especially what the secretary needs to prepare for each appointment or meeting • be realistic with the deadlines that are set to ensure that the secretary can complete all the allocated tasks well within the deadline • provide the necessary coaching if the secretary has made a mistake • be willing to assist the secretary if there is a crisis that the secretary may have to attend to • always praise the secretary for a job well done as this will motivate the secretary to maintain a high work etiquette.

It is important that a secretary be tactful and charming. If a secretary must apologise on behalf of the manager, the apology should be sincere and honest. Others will see the apology as a sign of professionalism and this will reflect positively on the manager and the organisation.

DEFINITION

contrast – compare two people or things to show the differences between them

1.4.6 Advantages of effective teamwork in the workplace

As previously mentioned, the manager and the secretary/management assistant are a team within the organisation and they need to understand what the advantages of teamwork are:

- Information is shared instantly.
- The work can be shared between team members.
- Each team member can contribute a different skill or talent that helps the team operate better. Decisions can be made with all team members providing input in the decision
- Problems that are identified can be discussed within the team and a solution can be found.

Figure 1.16 The team support and encourages each other.

- The manager can delegate different tasks or activities within the team.
- The output of a team can be more than what everyone could deliver individually (**synergy**).
- Working in a team helps team members be more focussed and results driven. They share the same goal and help to achieve it.
- The team can take on greater risks than they would have done individually.
- The team supports and encourages each other.
- Effective teams will help to develop effective leaders as team members can learn from each other.
- Individuals can develop a network of contacts within the team and will be able to use it after the team has broken up.
- Tasks can be completed quicker by teams as more can be done at the same time.
- Teamwork encourages more creativity and innovation from team members.
- Teamwork can boost staff morale especially where team members are having fun within the project.

> **Flashback to N4:** In Module 1 of *Office Practice* N4 you were introduced to the concept of teamwork in a business environment. You learned about the aim of teamwork in business, as well as the importance of team members being assigned roles and responsibilities. Go back to your N4 notes and revise what you learned.

Power break 1.5 GROUP WORK

In a group discuss the following:
1 The role of the manager towards the secretary.
2 The role of the secretary/management assistant towards the manager.

DEFINITION

synergy – the combined power of a group of things when they are working together that is greater than the total power achieved by each working separately

WHAT DO WE KNOW AND WHERE TO NEXT?

This first module covered the different managerial levels in a vertical and horizontal organisation structure with the help of organisation charts that explains these levels. We gained insight on the informal organisation and how this assists the organisation. We then reviewed the different functions of management in an organisation and how much time is spent on these functions at the different levels of management. We now understand the characteristics of a good manager and why it is important for the secretary to understand the roles of the manager. We also covered the functions of a secretary at the highest level of the hierarchy of the secretarial field. We concluded the module by contrasting the role of the secretary with that of the managers.

Module 2 explores the electronic office and includes aspects such as office automation, the impact of the microcomputer, and the internet.

Revisiting the learning objectives

Now that you have completed this module you should have achieved the learning objectives listed in the table below.

Learning objective	What you have learned	✔
With the aid of an organisation chart explain the levels of management in a small business enterprise under the vertical and horizontal perspectives.	A vertical organisation structure consists of top-, middle- and lower-levels of management. • The higher in the structure the more authority and accountability. • Communication and decisions are usually top down. • In a horizontal organisational structure, business is structured according to branches or departments. • The branch/department has the authority and accountability. • Communication and decisions are quicker as it is at department or branch level.	☐
Briefly explain the nature and function of the informal organisation.	The informal structure is not based on hierarchy or structure but based on social and cultural preferences of staff. Also known as the grapevine.	☐
Briefly elucidate on the functions of management with special reference to the function of general management and the skills required on the different levels of management.	The functions of management include planning, leading/activating, organising, co-ordinating, controlling and staffing. The skills required by all levels of management include technical skill (job knowledge), human skill (work with people) and conceptual skills (ideas and problem solving).	☐
Briefly explain why it is necessary for a secretary/management assistant to know the role of the manager.	The secretary should understand the role of the manager to assist the manager to achieve the goals and objectives within the organisation.	☐

continued on next page ...

Learning objective	What you have learned	✔
Explain the role of managers in a business enterprise.	The role of the manager has an impact on the following areas: • formulating the vision, mission and policy • implementing organisation and methods • making decisions on systems, processes, equipment and machinery • dealing with staff. Managers also have environmental responsibilities.	☐
Briefly explain the functions of a secretary/management assistant at the highest level of the hierarchy of secretarial posts.	The functions of the secretary at the highest level of the hierarchy of secretarial posts includes main activities (e.g. liaison, communication, correspondence), subsidiary activities (e.g., compiling reports and preparing correspondence), and general tasks (e.g., filing, typing/computer, reception). The characteristics of a successful secretary include efficiency, discreetness, flexibility, enthusiasm, loyalty and cheerfulness.	☐
Contrast the role of the secretary/management assistant with that of the manager.	The role of the secretary is to: • assist the manager • assist customers • assist other secretaries and work colleagues. The secretary must understand the manager's roles within the organisation, as well as the goals and objectives of the manager. The secretary should assist the manager to achieve success in the organisation. The manager, in turn, must provide leadership, coaching and guidance to the secretary.	☐

Assessment

1. Multiple choice

Choose the correct answer from the various options provided. Choose only A, B, C or D and write it next to the question number.

1.1 There are _____ levels of management in the management function.

    A   five

    B   two

    C   three

    D   four   (2)

1.2 Facilitating the procedures for specific activities is one of the following functions of management:

    A   planning

    B   organising

    C   leading

    D   controlling   (2)

1.3 The lowest level of management in the management function is _____ .

    A   the operating management

    B   top management

    C   the employees

    D   middle management   (2)

1.4 A horizontal organisational structure can be set up according to _____ .

    A   geographical regions

    B   customer segments

    C   functional departments

    D   all the above   (2)

1.5 To be successful in any enterprise a manager needs _____.

    A   technical skills

    B   human skills

    C   conceptual skills

    D   all the above   (2)

                      (5 × 2 = 10)

                      [10]

2. True or false

Choose whether the following statements are true or false. Write down the number of the question and 'true' or 'false'.

2.1 A vertical organisation structure consists of top-, middle- and lower-level management.

2.2 A horizontal organisational structure is based on different branches.

2.3 An informal organisation is governed by levels of authority.

2.4 Leadership means not to influence others' goals.

2.5 Environmental responsibilities are also one of the manager's roles.

                      (5 × 2 = 10)

                      [10]

3. Match the columns

Choose a description from Column B that matches the word/item in Column A. Write only the letter (A–E) next to the question number.

Column A	Column B
3.1 A manager	A. Managing the manager's diary
3.2 Delegation	B. The person who undertakes the responsibility of managing the enterprise
3.3 Confidential information	C. Answering telephone calls
3.4 Liaison	D. To transfer a task to someone else to complete
3.5 Formulate vision, mission and policy	E. Part of the manager's role

$(5 \times 2 = 10)$

[10]

4. Short questions

4.1 List five characteristics of:

    4.1.1 a secretary $(5 \times 1 = 5)$

    4.1.2 a good manager $(5 \times 1 = 5)$

4.2 Give six general tasks a secretary can assist with. $(6 \times 1 = 6)$

4.3 Provide the four divisions a secretary's roles can be divided into. $(4 \times 1 = 4)$

[20]

5. Discussion questions

5.1 Discuss the role of the manager towards the secretary. $(4 \times 2 = 8)$

5.2 Discuss the role of the secretary/management assistant towards the manager. $(4 \times 2 = 8)$

5.3 Discuss the management functions of the supervisor using the following headings:

    5.3.1 Planning $(2 \times 2 = 4)$

    5.3.2 Organising $(2 \times 2 = 4)$

    5.3.3 Activating $(2 \times 2 = 4)$

    5.3.4 Controlling $(2 \times 2 = 4)$

5.4 Discuss nine important points a management assistant/secretary should keep in mind when doing work for two managers. $(9 \times 2 = 18)$

[50]

Grand total: 100 marks

MODULE 2

THE ELECTRONIC OFFICE

This module considers the following aspects of the electronic office environment:

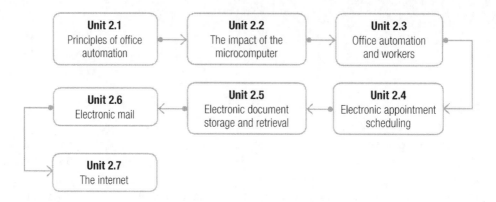

Unit 2.1
Principles of office automation

Unit 2.2
The impact of the microcomputer

Unit 2.3
Office automation and workers

Unit 2.6
Electronic mail

Unit 2.5
Electronic document storage and retrieval

Unit 2.4
Electronic appointment scheduling

Unit 2.7
The internet

Learning objectives

After completing this module, you should be able to do the following:
- Define the concept office automation, name the principles it is based on and briefly elucidate on its effect on the secretary/management assistant.
- Briefly explain how technological developments have contributed to office automation and how these have made the integration of electronic equipment possible.
- List the applications of computer technology in the business world and elucidate the impact thereof on the lives of the customers.
- List the applications of microcomputers in the wider community and particularly in business enterprises and briefly elucidate the impact thereof on the lives of office workers in general and secretaries/management assistants in particular.
- Briefly elucidate on the ergonomics of the electronic office.
- List and briefly explain the basic elements of the electronic office and the implications of office automation.
- Explain how office automation effects office layout, desktop arrangements, work routine and list the positive and negative effect it has on office workers.
- Briefly explain the key features of an electronic diary and list the points to be considered in choosing an appropriate electronic appointment-scheduling program.

continued on next page ...

Learning objectives

- Briefly elucidate on the advantages of an electronic diary compared to the traditional diary.
- Briefly explain the concept of 'the paper-less office/electronic office' and point out how it differs from the traditional filing system.
- Compare the different media for electronic document/data storage, elucidate on the advantages and disadvantages thereof and motivate the use of back-up copies.
- Explain the coding and labelling of diskettes and, given a case study on types of information to be stored on diskettes, propose the proper coding and labelling for such information.
- Propose an effective filing system for diskettes in diskette holders/storage boxes.
- Compare an electronic and traditional filing index system regarding accessibility, time to look up index, speed of recovery/retrieval and updating.
- Briefly explain the concepts of computeroutput-microfilm (COM) and computer-assisted retrieval (CAR) as methods of electronic documents storage and retrieval linked to a microform system.
- Define the concept of electronic mail (email) and explain the following in this connection:
  - communication devices
  - data links
  - protocol or specifications
  - applications/uses
  - advantages and disadvantages
  - forms of email.

Key terms

automation (office)	merge	SD card
binary	network server	software
cloud storage	optical disk	spreadsheet
data link	protocol	
flash drive	random-access memory	
hard disk drive (HDD)	(RAM)	
hardware	read-only memory (ROM)	

Starting point

Verushna continues with her development in the corporate sector. Her mentor, Roland Coetzee, is helping her get a better understanding of the electronic office. Roland explains that all organisations, regardless of their size, seek to find a competitive edge in the marketplace. When it comes down to the wire, the deriving a competitive edge can come from automated processes that make an office run much smoother. Within the context of an automated office, several key elements play an important role in making the office an effective mechanism in the fight to get ahead in the marketplace. Concepts like a 'paper-less office' or 'electronic storage and retrieval system' help make office automation a topic that requires, especially, the secretary/management assistant to look at and to help management gain insight into the benefits of office automation.

Figure 2.1 Verushna's mentor has shown her how automation can make an organisation more effective.

UNIT 2.1 **Principles of office automation**

Office **automation** refers to the process of streamlining normal office administration activities by using automatic steps to replace other manual processes.

> **Did you know?** During the 1900s the secretary would type up letters for the manager using a typewriter. With the invention of the personal computer in 1975, the secretary can now do this activity on the computer and add in pictures and other information that was not possible on the typewriter.

Figure 2.2 In the past, office workers used typewriters and before that handwritten notes.

2.1.1 What is office automation?

Office automation replaces manual processes with automatic methods. It allows us to do large volumes of work quicker and more accurately. For example, in the past, the business would complete a cheque to pay someone and the person would then have to go to the bank or an ATM to deposit the cheque. With the advent of internet, banking, it is possible for the business to pay the money directly from their bank account into the bank account of the person who they want to pay; this is known as electronic funds transfer.

> **DEFINITION**
>
> **automation (office)** – introducing computerised steps to replace a manual process

The principles of office automation are the following:

- There are quicker and easier ways of doing repetitive tasks.
- You need less workers to perform certain tasks.
- There is less space needed to store documents as it can be stored electronically.
- Office automation can free up the office workers' time to focus on other tasks.

2.1.2 The effects of office automation on the secretary/ management assistant

Table 2.1 gives some examples of how office automation has had a positive impact on the work of the secretary/management assistant.

Table 2.1 Examples of office automation and its impact on the work

Example of office automation	Impact on the work
Email autoresponders	If someone sends an email to the business email address and an automatic reply goes to the sender saying something like 'thank you for contacting ABC Pty (Ltd), one of trained staff will contact you shortly to assist with your query'. This means that the secretary does not have to manually reply to each email that is received.
Integrated voice recognition	When you phone a company, the automatic response could be, 'Please press one for enquiries, two for finance, three for sales, or nine for the switchboard'. The system then directs the call to the right department to help the caller.
Online questionnaires	As the person types the answers in a questionnaire, it is added automatically to other responses received. This makes it easier to analyse the data.
Adding a speed dial on a telephone	You can programme a telephone number into the telephone. Instead of dialling the full number, you only dial the speed dial code (shortened number) to call the person.
Mail **merge**	When a standard letter needs to be sent to many recipients, the secretary can type up the mailing information for each recipient or use a spreadsheet or other database where the contact information is kept and add this information automatically as each letter is printed.
Outsourcing	Outsourcing entails transferring a business activity to someone else who is more skilled or equipped for that specific activity. For example, if the secretary is going online to make travel bookings or booking hotel accommodation, the business can request a travel agent to make the bookings for them. The secretary only communicates with the travel agent to ensure that the bookings are completed.

> **DEFINITION**
>
> **merge** – to join data from direct sources

2.1.3 How changes in technology have helped office automation

Technological changes, such as advances in **hardware**, software, digital systems and **data links**, have been at the centre of office automation. Large and small organisations and businesses are continuously looking at how technology can change the way they work.

Figure 2.3 Is there a better way to do this activity?

Hardware

Advances in technology, such as those listed below, has resulted in hardware becoming much smaller, lighter and faster.

- The creation of the laptop or notebook computer that has made it possible to take information physically to a customer, supplier or banker.
- The invention of the cellphone has made it possible to make and receive phone calls, emails and instant messages from virtually anywhere in the world.
- Improvements in connectivity, such as fibre to the business (FTTB) or fibre to the home (FTTH), has made it possible to send and receive vast amounts of data at much faster speeds than was possible with older technology like the postal service.
- The scanning of documents has reduced the need to physically store documents, thus ensuring that there is less paper in the office environment.
- Improvements in capacity of both the computer hard drive and central processing unit (CPU) has made the actual physical drive smaller. These smaller drives can store much more data than was previously possible.

Figure 2.4 Advances in technology have made the computer smaller and faster.

- Integrated voice recognition allows callers to be directed to the right person or department as it offers choices (see examples in Table 2.1 above).

> **DEFINITIONS**
>
> **hardware** – the physical components of a computer
> **data link** – a telecommunications link that can send or receive data

Software

As with hardware, **software** has also evolved to perform complex tasks much quicker. The main thrust of the software changes comes from advances in the programming used to develop the software. Examples of changes in software include the following:

- Internet browsers, such as Mozilla Firefox, Google Chrome and Internet Explorer, are constantly changing the way pictures, data and videos are stored. It is also possible to open an internet session much quicker.
- Email programs, such Outlook or Gmail, allow users to send and receive complex emails that can contain pictures, videos, presentations, documents, and suchlike.
- Word processing applications, such as Microsoft Word and Apple Pages, as well as text editing programmes, such as Microsoft Notepad, allow users to create documents, certificates, business cards, invoices and many other types and styles of documents.
- Microsoft PowerPoint allows user to create presentations that contain data, graphs, videos, pictures, and so on.
- Microsoft Excel gives users the ability to do complex calculations and store large amounts of data that can be summarised in tables or **spreadsheets**.
- Microsoft Access is used to store large databases that can then be used to capture data or extract reports that a business can use.
- Cortana, Siri and Google Assistant are software programs that allow users to give verbal instructions to the computer or cellphone and can even provide feedback, either audibly or in writing. For example, if you say to Cortana 'what is the weather in Durban today?', it will reply with 'Today is 28 degrees with a 60% chance of rain'.

Other examples of automated solutions provided by software include (among others) email autoresponders, online questionnaires and mail merge.

Digital systems

In the automated office environment, the organisation will rely on digital systems. Digital systems is the technology that the computer is based on. Digital systems use a **binary** system to store data as either 0 or 1 (zero or one). The computer interprets the combinations of zeros or ones to represent a letter, number or a symbol. For example, 010101 could be a '3' for a computer. Computer programming languages take the letters, numbers and symbols that humans understand and convert these into their binary equivalent so that the computer understands what it is that we are typing.

> **DEFINITIONS**
>
> **software** – the programs used by a computer
> **spreadsheet** – a document in which data is arranged across rows and columns allowing the data to be calculated and/or analysed
> **binary** – made up of two digits

Data links

Data links are the links used in telecommunication to share information. This is like a telephone system with a transmitter and a receiver joined together to share information. This technology helps to speed up data transmission to give the organisation a marginal advantage over competitors that rely on outdated technology.

2.1.4 Integration of electronic equipment in work

The rapid advances in hardware, software, digital systems and data links has made electronic equipment, such as computers, all-in-one printers, projectors, speaker telephones and cellphones, important parts of the automated office environment. The office environment has benefitted from these advances and needs less space for all the paper that a manual office environment generated.

Figure 2.5 The effect of virtual reality and other technological advancements shape the working environment.

> **Did you know?** An all-in-one printer allows a user to print, scan, fax, copy and, in some cases, even access the internet.

Power break 2.1 INDIVIDUAL WORK

Connect the word(s) in Column A with a matching description in Column B

Column A	Column B
1. Outsourcing	A. Automatic response system that directs calls to the right department
2. Email autoresponders	B. When a business allows activities to be done by other people or businesses who are more skilled
3. Mail merge	C. Links that are used in telecommunications to share information
4. Integrated voice recognition	D. Where the same standard letter is sent to many recipients
5. Adding a speed dial on a telephone	E. When an email is sent to the business and an automatic reply goes to the sender
6. Online questionnaires	F. Programme numbers in the phone instead of dialling the full number every time
7. Integration of electronic equipment	G. Where software, digital systems, data links and all-in-one printers are part of the office environment
8. Data links	H. Complete information online to make data analysis easier

UNIT 2.2 The impact of the microcomputer

Microcomputers have been instrumental in helping to automate certain processes in the modern office environment. The improvements in technology have helped customers, the wider community, office workers and secretaries/management assistants in various ways.

2.2.1 The application of microcomputer technology in business and its impact on customers

A microcomputer (a term formerly used for a personal computer), is a device that has microprocessors, **random-access memory (RAM)**, **read-only memory (ROM)**, and input devices, such as a mouse/keyboard/stylus/scanner, which send the information to an output device, such as a screen and printer. Figure 2.6 shows these components.

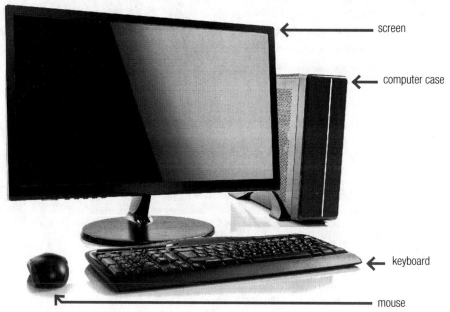

Figure 2.6 The components of a microcomputer.

Micro-computers in the business world
In the business world, microcomputers are used:
* as a communication tool, such as websites, email, newsletters, or social media platforms (Facebook, Twitter, etc.)

> **DEFINITIONS**
>
> **random-access memory (RAM)** – the physical hardware inside a computer that temporarily stores data, serving as the computer's 'working' memory.
>
> **read-only memory (ROM)** – the memory from which we can only read but cannot write on it; the information is stored permanently in such memories during manufacture.

- for internet browsing, which allows a business to advertise and/or sell its products and services to customers and prospective employees
- to create documents, such as contracts, pamphlets, business reports and proposals
- to create spreadsheets and databases to analyse customer, supplier or other wider community data
- to record transactions, such as orders, delivery notes, invoices and credit notes
- to create presentations to share with customers, suppliers, employees, investors, and others
- to store and retrieve electronic documents
- as a training tool using videos, books, or other training material.

Impact of microcomputer technology on the lives of office workers

Microcomputer technology has affected office workers in numerous ways:

- The technology provides the office workers, secretaries/management assistants with opportunities for career development.
- The workers can gain the necessary skills and knowledge they need to work in their current or future positions.
- The technology makes it easier to communicate with customers, suppliers, colleagues, government, community and other stakeholders.
- The technology provides a professional approach to customer service if the output is in a user-friendly format that is easily accessible to the customer.
- Research and development initiatives are improved where the office workers can use the microcomputer to gain insights on new technology.
- Work is completed at a faster pace than using the manual approach by applying automated solutions on the microcomputer

Customer benefits from businesses using the microcomputer

A customer can use a microcomputer to:

- find suppliers
- open new accounts
- maintain customer contact information
- discover new products and services
- compare prices between different suppliers of the same product
- place orders with suppliers
- track progress on deliveries
- receive invoices and statements
- make payments to suppliers and service providers
- log product returns and/or queries
- communicate with the business
- locate the business' head office or different branches
- find the contact information of the business.

2.2.2 Applications of microcomputer technology in the wider community

Amongst other things, the wider community can use microcomputers to:

- find suppliers and customers
- find employment opportunities
- advertise available positions to attract new employees
- offer bursaries and scholarships to deserving students
- offer sponsorship for sports teams and/or sports men/women
- find investment opportunities
- find new sources of funding
- advertise products and services
- share information of the business
- submit statutory requirements, for example, unemployment insurance, income tax, and value added tax submissions
- publish financial statements and other business reports
- respond to news or events that involve the business
- keep up-to-date with changes in technology
- keep abreast of developments in industry
- provide capacity building opportunities for employees
- offer training programmes that can help communities
- interact with communities and institutions that the business deals with.

Power break 2.2   INDIVIDUAL WORK

Roland has asked Verushna to write an article for the organisation's newsletter explaining the key advantages that microcomputers offer customers. Draw up an article to assist Verushna to complete this assignment.

UNIT 2.3 **Office automation and workers**

In this unit, we will turn our attention to how office automation influences the work environment of office workers.

2.3.1 Ergonomics

Flashback to N5: *Office Practice* N5 discussed ergonomics in an office. Go back to your notes to refresh your memory.

Ergonomics is defined as 'ensuring that the worker can have the right office layout with the right furniture and equipment where the lighting, airflow, ventilation and noise levels are set up in such a way that he/she can work as productively as possible'.

Despite having good office ergonomics, a worker could still suffer from fatigue, also referred to as 'office syndrome'. This fatigue affects work productivity. Figure 2.7 shows how to sit correctly at a computer, and so avoid the dangers of fatigue.

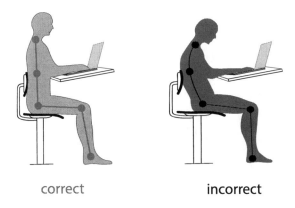

correct   incorrect

Figure 2.7 How to sit correctly when working at a computer.

2.3.2 Basic elements of the electronic office

The electronic office or 'e-office' refers to an office environment where there is greater reliance on the use of computers and/or computer-aided technologies to help office workers to be more productive. Given the essence of the e-office, we can use computers to control things such as lighting, airflow, ventilation, and noise levels.

Figure 2.8 The modern office worker has lots of electronic equipment operating simultaneously.

2.3.3 Implications of office automation

This section considers some of the many aspects of business affected by the increase in office automation.

Human resource requirements

The automation of the office environment has both positive and negative impacts on office workers. On the positive side, workers have become more productive. However, on the negative side, certain lower-level office jobs have become unnecessary (redundant) resulting in job losses.

Communication links

Office automation has resulted in faster lines of communication. Workers can contact managers, suppliers, customers and other stakeholders much easier using automated communication methods. This is especially evident in offices using fibre optic cables for data connections. The transfer of data is now more reliable and faster data than with the traditional copper cable lines of communication.

Provision and maintenance of equipment and furniture

In an automated office environment, the provision and maintenance of equipment and furniture has moved from a manually recorded requisition system to a system that automatically creates and sends through a purchase order to a supplier. For example, if a secretary needs a new chair, a requisition for the new chair automatically goes to the manager for approval. Once approved, the requisition is sent to the buying department to order the new chair or it is automatically sent to the pre-approved supplier to supply the new chair.

Temperature control

Automatic office temperature control, which maintains the ideal office temperature, has made it more comfortable for office workers resulting in improved productivity.

Lighting

Improvements in the brightness, durability of light bulbs as well as the automation of lighting systems has resulted in a more pleasant and productive office environment.

> **Did you know?** Lumens are measurements of the brightness of a light. For example, a 100 W light bulb will give off 1 600 lumens of light, whereas a 40 W light bulb only gives off 450 lumens of light.

Figure 2.9 Modern lighting in a boardroom

Control of static electricity

As small children, we all thought that generating static electricity was harmless fun, especially if we dragged our feet on the carpet and then touched our brother, sister, or a friend to give them a mild shock. In an office environment, static electricity can lead to damaged computers and other equipment. Installing an automatic humidifier can help to control the humidity in the office and help to reduce the amount of static electricity in the office environment.

Security information

The introduction of automated security systems has led to a safer and more secure work environment.

Supervision

The automation of the office environment has given management a more reliable way of monitoring and evaluating the workflow of workers.

2.3.4 Effects of office automation on workplace layout and work routine

Office automation not only benefits the office worker directly but also has an impact on the set up of the office layout and desktop arrangement, and the work routine that the office workers must follow.

Office layout

The automation of the office has led to very effective home and virtual office environments. Even the traditional, cubicle and open plan office layouts have become more effective and more productive work environments.

> **Flashback to N5:** *Office Practice* N5, Module 1 discussed various office layout styles (traditional, open plan, cubicle, home office and virtual office).

Figure 2.10 An airy, well-lit home office with all office equipment close at hand will be a productive workspace.

In addition, the way that the workstation is organised can help improve productivity. For example, if the secretary needs to print confidential documents for the manager it would be better to position the printer at or close to the secretary's workstation. This will allow the confidential information to be easily and quickly collected.

Desktop arrangements

As most office workers spend much of their day working on a computer, the arrangement of the desktop becomes more significant. Selecting a calming wallpaper, lock screen and screen saver can help the worker be more productive. There are even claims that certain colours help improve memory. The arrangement of the equipment and other tools can also help the office worker be more productive. Although the changes can help improve productivity they could also result in lower staff morale if the wrong set up is selected.

Work routine

A work routine describes the steps followed to achieve a specific task. For example, when requesting stationery for a new employee, the manager completes a requisition form that lists all the stationery items needed. The manager then approves the requisition and the secretary issues the stationery and updates the stationery stock record. With office automation, the manager sends the requisition electronically, the secretary updates the stationery stock record on the computer and can complete the process much quicker than if it was a manually-recorded system.

Power break 2.3   GROUP WORK

The following steps in the selling process are scrambled. As a group, rearrange the steps in the process in the correct order:
1. The sales clerk completes and sends a memo to the stock controller enquiring whether the items for sale are in stock.
2. If the items are in stock, the sales clerk prepares and faxes an order confirmation to buyer.
3. The delivery note and tax invoice is faxed to the buyer.
4. The sales clerk follows up the sale.
5. The buyer accepts the quotation and sends an order form.
6. The sales clerk receives the order form and proceeds to process the order.
7. The sales clerk prepares a delivery note and sends the white and yellow copies to the debtor's clerk in the finance department.
8. The debtor's clerk receives the delivery note and prepares a tax invoice.
9. The sales clerk receives the sales enquiry to prepare a quotation.
10. The sales clerk prepares and faxes the quotation to the prospective buyer.

UNIT 2.4 Electronic appointment scheduling

Office automation has influenced the ways that office workers and managers' schedule and deal with appointments. Here are some of the key features of an electronic appointment scheduler/electronic diary:

- An electronic diary allows a user to schedule appointments and tasks in an electronic calendar that is unique for each user.
- The electronic diary can be included in a software package like Microsoft Outlook or it could be web based like Google Calendar.
- The electronic diary views include a daily view, a weekly view, a monthly view, an agenda view, etc.
- An added feature of an electronic diary is that holidays are included for a specific country/countries.
- A reminder function alerts users of an upcoming calendar event, appointment or task that needs completing.
- There are also shared calendars that allow many people to access the same information.

Figure 2.11 Managing your time with an electronic diary

2.4.1 Choosing an electronic appointment-scheduling program

The choice of an appointment-scheduling program requires the user to decide on the following:

- How will the program be accessed (website, desktop computer, tablet, or cellphone)?
- Is the scheduling program compatible with the user's email account?
- Does the program display multiple time zones?
- Will changes made on one device be updated on all other devices?
- Does the scheduling program allow the user to grant access to the program? For example, the secretary should have access to the manager's diary.
- Can the scheduling programme gain access to the user's contact list to make it easier to schedule appointments?
- What are the security features of the scheduling software?

2.4.2 Advantages of electronic diaries

There are numerous advantages of using an electronic diary:

- Security: A user can electronically protect an electronic diary on a computer, tablet computer or cellphone. A manual diary needs to be locked away to keep it secure.
- Sharing: Users can easily share their electronic diary with anyone else. This is especially relevant for the managers who must share diaries with their secretary.

- Reminders and scheduling: Electronic diaries can provide timely reminders of upcoming appointments. Manual diaries rely on the user to constantly review the diary to see when appointments will take place.
- Edits and tracking: An electronic diary makes it possible to make simultaneously changes to appointments and update all the attendees for a meeting. For a manual diary, each attendee must be contacted individually to advise them of any changes.
- Time zones: In a global market, people need to understand time difference when scheduling international meetings or phone calls. An electronic diary can show multiple time zones, which makes it easier to schedule meetings at the optimal time for all parties involved.

Power break 2.4 GROUP WORK

In a group, list at least five disadvantages of using a manual diary and compare how an electronic diary helps to overcome those disadvantages.

UNIT 2.5 Electronic document storage and retrieval

This unit focuses on the paper-less office and electronic document storage and retrieval.

2.5.1 The 'paper-less' office

A paper-less office is an office that has reduced or even eliminated the need for paper. This is achieved by using technology, such as scanning or electronic forms, to convert the paper digitally. In South Africa, the South African Revenue Service (SARS) serves as a good example of moving to a paper-less office with the introduction of e-filing. Customers can now lodge their tax returns using e-filing instead of having to manually submit these forms at a tax office.

2.5.2 Electronic filing and index systems compared to traditional systems

The requirements of a good filing system are simplicity, neatness, economy, suitability, safety, durability, flexibility and retention.

Flashback to N4: When comparing electronic filing and indexing systems with traditional filing and index systems, reflect back on Module 7 of *Office Practice* N4, which covers the requirements of a good filing system.

Now let us compare an electronic filing and indexing system with a traditional filing and indexing system based on the requirements of a good filing and indexing system mentioned above.

Table 2.2 An electronic filing and indexing system compared to a traditional filing and indexing system

Criteria	Electronic filing and indexing system	Traditional filing and indexing system
Simplicity	Users who understand the system can access files.	Files are accessible to all office staff.
Neatness	Files remain neat and tidy within the filing system structure.	Files can become very untidy if they are accessed on a regular basis.
Economy	The system can be expensive to set up and maintain but does not occupy floor space.	Equipment, paper and the files can take up valuable floor space in the office.
Suitability	The system can be difficult to apply to all businesses.	The system is suitable for all businesses.
Safety	Files are safe from physical dangers but exposed to digital dangers, such as hacking and viruses.	Files may not be safe from physical dangers, such as fire, dust, burglars and insects.
Durability	Files can be kept for the lifespan of the equipment used for storing.	Some documents, such as fax copies, can fade after a few months or years.
Flexibility	Files can be stored on different media, so they can be used on different users' computers. Files are easily shared between users.	The system is not very flexible.
Retention	Files can be kept for the lifespan of the equipment used for storing.	Files can be kept for the lifespan of the paper or will be shredded after their retention date, whichever comes first.

2.5.3 Comparison of different electronic document storage media

Documents can be stored electronically on various media, each with its own advantages and disadvantages.

Diskette

In the past, diskettes were used to save user files and folders on a removable storage media. This was largely popular in the 1990s when microcomputers were all fitted with drives to read this media. There were two types of diskettes: floppy disks and stiffy disks.

A floppy disk (also called a 'floppy') is a type of disk storage composed of a disk of thin and flexible magnetic storage medium, sealed in a rectangular plastic enclosure. Floppy disks were phased out rapidly when stiffy disks became the accepted standard. A 'stiffy' was simply a 3.5-inch floppy disc that came in a stiffer, less flexible plastic 'envelope' or case.

Figure 2.12 A stiffy disk.

Hard disk drive

All computers need a **hard disk drive (HDD)** to operate and store user's programmes and files. The drive uses magnetic storage to store data. HDDs are more reliable than diskettes as they can be built into the computer. There are three main types namely: a solid state hard drive, external hard drive or internal hard drive. A hard drive allows users to save information, erase it, and then save other information in its place. An external hard drive is widely believed to be the best for data backups for a personal computer.

Network server

A **network server** is found on a local area network (LAN) where different users all gain access to the same computer hard drive to access shared files and folders. This is useful for sharing information within a closed group. Version control can become a problem when saving files to a network server as two or more people can download a copy of the master file at the same time. Each one can make changes to the file, but when it is uploaded back onto the network server some information can be lost as only the changes made by the last user will reflect on the network server copy.

Optical disk

An **optical disk**/CD-ROM/DVD-ROM is similar to the stiffy diskette but works on laser technology. A low-power laser 'burns' information onto the CD/DVD by. These discs are generally regarded as a reliable source, especially for backups. They are susceptible to damage from falling or bending if left in the sun. An optical disc is considered a removable data storage device.

Magnetic tape

Magnetic tapes work on the same principle of a hard drive where data is transferred onto the tape using magnets. They allow users to store vast amounts of data onto the magnetic strip that is kept on a reel.

> **DEFINITIONS**
>
> **hard disk drive (HDD)** – a computer hardware device that permanently stores and retrieves data on a computer
>
> **network server** – a computer system, which is used as the central repository of data and various programs that are shared by users in a network
>
> **optical disk** – an electronic data storage medium that can be written to and read using a low-powered laser beam

Cloud storage

Cloud storage is like a network server as it allows users to share data and information that is stored remotely. The cloud can be located anywhere in the world. With recent incidents involving hacking of private information kept in cloud storage, people have become reluctant to store private information in the cloud.

Figure 2.13 Examples of storage media.

USB flash drive

A USB **flash drive** is a smaller version of an external hard drive. These drives vary in size from 1 gigabyte (GB) up to versions that can be as big as 1 terabyte (TB), which is 1 024 GB. They are useful if you need to access files only temporarily. One disadvantage is that a flash drive is small and can easily be lost.

Did you know? There are plans to create a USB flash drive that can store 2 TB of data. This is big enough for backup copies of two or more personal computers.

DEFINITIONS

cloud storage – online space that you use to store your data, photos, music, and videos for access from any of your devices

flash drive – a small piece of equipment used to store and transfer information for computers using a USB

Memory card

A memory card is a smaller version of a stiffy disk and is typically used in digital cameras and video cameras.

SD card

SD cards are currently the smallest storage medium and are used in cellphones and tablet computers.

2.5.4 Advantages and disadvantages of electronic document storage

Table 2.3 gives some of the advantages and disadvantages of electronic document storage.

Table 2.3 Advantages and disadvantages of electronic document storage

Advantages	Disadvantages
It uses less paper.	It may be costlier to maintain a computer filing system especially if it uses cloud storage that is billed based on the amount of data stored in the cloud.
It uses less storage space for paper filing.	Documents are only available if the computer system is online.
It has lower printing costs.	There may be job losses for workers responsible for document filing and retrieval of paper documents.
Small businesses use less electricity as they use less printers, fax machines, etc.	Staff needs to be trained on how to use the filing system, this can be costly and takes time to complete.
Businesses could have a lower carbon footprint from using less paper.	Online systems are always vulnerable to computer hacking and viruses. This could lead to sensitive company information landing in the wrong hands or disappearing.
It is easier to trace documents in an electronic system.	If the business does not have a back-up system, it may lose important data if the system crashes.
	Sharing documents could result in data loss if there are insufficient controls in place.

DEFINITION

SD card – an ultra-small flash memory card designed to provide high-capacity memory in a small size; used in many small portable devices

2.5.5 Coding and labelling of electronically stored documents

All electronically stored documents need a system that allows authorised users to gain access to the documents. When looking at the coding and labelling of electronically stored documents, the business needs to take note of the following:

- Only authorised users should have access to the folders where documents are stored.
- Where there are multiple users accessing the same data, it is important that the data is stored on a shared folder or on a server.
- The business should have a policy in place that explains who has access to sensitive data held on shared folders/server.
- Access to shared folders/server can be password controlled to prevent unauthorised access to sensitive information.
- The business can create a file classification system to help staff identify where documents are stored. This would be like the Dewey system used in libraries where books are stored by subject and by author. Each subject is allocated a code and each book within a subject is filed alphanumerically to show the user where to find the book in the library. The book then has the code on its spine and can be found easily.
- Certain computer programs allow more than one user to make changes to a document at a time. However, there need to be clear rules on whose data is accepted if two users update the same record but with different information.
- For documents that are not shared, the system should advise a second user trying to access a document that it is currently in use and can only be opened as a 'Read-only' document.

Coding and labelling systems include computer-assisted retrieval (CAR) and computer output microfilm (COM).

CAR is a document and retrieval system that uses computerised indexing, bar coding and reading technologies to help with document storage and retrieval. The bar codes used in major supermarkets are examples of CAR. The bar code reader reads the bar code and looks up the product information and price, and then outputs this to the computer screen. Each product has a unique bar code and this information is stored on a central database (network server) in the supermarket.

COM converts electronic documents (data) onto microfilm to archive documents.

2.5.6 Storage media filing system

Any filing system requires an index that helps users to find documents easily. A storage media filing system (including diskettes, magnetic tapes, USB flash drives, etc.) should include the following:

- The system should have a standard policy for labelling the storage media. This is applicable to media that allows the user to write on the media.
- The date system used on the label should be consistent to allow for easier storage and retrieval. It should be physically stuck to the media.

- The media should be kept in a safe and secure location away from direct sunlight and magnets as these could damage the storage media. Optical disks are best stored in paper sleeves to protect them from dust.
- Small storage media can be filed in a plastic container that allows for easy access and retrieval.
- The system can be sub-divided into the various sections based on the organisation's index system.

Power break 2.5   INDIVIDUAL WORK

As the secretary, you are tasked to research a filing system that could be implemented in the organisation. Which one of the two filing systems will benefit the company most: an electronic filing system or a traditional filing system? Motivate your answer.

UNIT 2.6 Electronic mail (email)

Electronic mail (email) is a way of communicating with anyone who has an email address and is the newest and fastest way of sending and receiving messages. Email has made it much easier to send messages, pictures, figures or other information to other people. With email, you can send parts of documents or the entire document, as long as it does not exceed the maximum size of an email as indicated by the internet service provider (ISP).

Figure 2.14 Email is the most used tool for communication.

2.6.1 Communication devices

Briefly, a communication device can send and receive an analogue or digital signal over the telephone, using fibre optic cable or wirelessly. WiFi routers, modems and USB dongles are examples of communication devices.

2.6.2 Data links

A data link is a telecommunications link that can send or receive data. On example of this is a USB modem (USBB dongle) that can be plugged into a laptop to connect it to the internet. The ISP will broadcast the internet signal on different channels and the data link device must be set up on the correct channel to successfully connect to the internet. There are various data link devices, including modems, wireless (WiFi) routers and LTE routers:

- A modem (modulator–demodulator) is a device to connect to the internet over a telephone connection.
- A WiFi router is a device connected to a special telephone line used to connect other devices to the internet wirelessly.
- An LTE router is a device that connects to a cellular/mobile network and is used to connect other devices to the internet wirelessly.

2.6.3 Email protocols

Communication **protocols** are the set of procedures that apply when communicating. The most commonly used and supported email protocols are:

- Internet Message Access Protocol (IMAP)
- Post Office Protocol (POP3)
- Simple Message Transfer Protocol (SMTP).

Internet Message Access Protocol (IMAP)

When setting up an email account on a communication device, such as a computer, tablet computer, or cellphone, the user needs to obtain the IMAP settings from the relevant email service provider, such as Google Mail or Outlook.com. The IMAP address will tell the email programme, such as Outlook or Zimbra, to find the user's emails at the address provided. This is like the post office where all the mail is kept. IMAP emails are always stored on the server. The same messages will be displayed on different devices. For example, the email on your computer will be shown on your cellphone and tablet computer.

> **DEFINITION**
>
> **protocol –** a set of procedures that apply when communicating

Post Office Protocol (POP3)

Similar to IMAP, POP3 tells the email program where to retrieve the emails from. However, with POP3, when the email is downloaded to a computer, it stays on the computer unless the user has specified to leave a copy of the message on the server. This is like having your mail delivered to your home. So, the downloaded email is only available on the one device.

Simple Message Transfer Protocol (SMTP)

When sending out email messages, the email program needs an address to send the message to, but it also needs a specific transfer route that it must follow; this is called Simple Message Transfer Protocol (SMTP).

2.6.4 Applications/uses of email

The primary use of email is to exchange messages between two or more users. It is widely used for business communication. It is also used in advertising to alert customers of products or services that a supplier or service provider is offering, and as a tool to spread news headlines that contain links that take users to the appropriate website where the full article is available for the user to read.

2.6.5 Advantages and disadvantages of email

Table 2.4 provides an overview of the main advantages and disadvantages of email.

Table 2.4 Advantages and disadvantages of email

Advantages of email	Disadvantages of email
Email is simple, quick and convenient to use.	Email lacks a personal touch.
An email can be sent to multiple recipients at once.	The email application can give rise to unwanted emails.
An email can provide an audit trail of communication in a specific subject.	Email messages can be used to spread computer viruses that could harm your device.
Email allows users to search and find specific messages.	Email messages can take up a lot of storage space on smaller devices, such as cellphones and tablets.
Email messages are easily accessible from any device that has been set up to receive emails.	Email can interfere with a person's work life balance, especially if messages are sent outside of normal working hours.
The user can easily archive email messages.	There is a limit on the maximum size of the emails that can be sent.
Emails can be controlled and allowed to be moved to folders to make it easier to see and save important messages.	It is easy to send emails more than once.

continued on next page …

Advantages of email	Disadvantages of email
An out-of-office email can be set up to notify a recipient that the person the email has been sent to is on leave or travelling.	It can be overwhelming if a user receives too many emails.
Sending customer statements via email can save on printing and paper costs.	
A business can save on postal charges by sending marketing material via email.	

Power break 2.6   GROUP WORK

Your manager is the head of the Marketing Department of Cellphones Plus, a cellphone manufacturer. He needs to inform customers of a new cellphone range that will be available next week on Wednesday. The manager asks you to draft an email message to the customers giving them all the necessary information about the new cellphone range.

UNIT 2.7 **The internet**

Flashback to N4: Go back and read through to Module 2 of *Office Practice* N4, which explored the internet.

2.7.1 How does the internet work?

The internet or the World Wide Web is a system that allows computers from all around the world to connect and exchange information. Information is stored on websites. Anyone can set up a website, from large corporations to individuals. A website has one or several web pages linked to it. This website is then stored on a computer called a server.

Figure 2.15 Businesses and private individuals can use the internet to advertise and sell products.

Anyone can search for information on the internet using a search engine like Google, Ask or Bing. The search engine will offer possible matching websites for the user to access. Alternatively, the user can enter the web address for the website and can then access the information on the server. The server connection to the internet is through a data connection. The data connection can be done through fibre optic cables, telephone wires, satellite or mobile connection.

2.7.2 Benefits of the internet

These are some benefits of using the internet:

- We use the internet to access any information, knowledge and training on all topics.
- Electronic mail or email is sent and received using the internet.
- The internet allows access to live coverage of global news, events and market data.
- Businesses or individuals can use the internet for buying, advertising and selling products and services online.
- The internet provides online maps with live traffic information, which allows users to plan trips more effectively.
- The internet allows social interaction with people across the globe.
- The internet provides access to online storage and back up of important information.
- The internet provides access to online entertainment stored as music or videos

2.7.3 Forms of internet uses

The internet can be used for the following applications:

- email
- streaming media
- social interaction
- information sharing
- cloud computing
- communication, including video, Voice over Internet Protocol (VoIP) or text.

Electronic mail

As we discussed in the previous unit, email is a way of communicating with anyone who has an email address. With the introduction of email, the sending of messages, pictures, figures or other information between people was made much easier. With email you can send parts of documents or the entire document as long as it does not exceed the maximum size of an email as indicated by the internet service provider.

Streaming media

An internet connection allows users to watch videos or full-length movies or listen to music. Services such as YouTube or Vimeo allow users to watch or download short videos on various topics; whereas a service like Apple music or Deezer allows the user listen to and download single tracks of music or even entire albums.

Social interaction

The internet allows users to interact socially with friends, family or followers on platforms such as Facebook, Twitter and Instagram. Users can post videos, audio clips, news, messages and photos on these social media platforms.

Information sharing

As much as the internet provides good entertainment and social interaction, it is also a powerful tool for sharing information. It can be used to provide training material to users spread across the globe. It is also an important source of local and international news.

Cloud computing

Services such as iCloud for Windows, Google Drive or Dropbox allow internet users to store documents, photos, videos or audio files on the internet. The user can then grant other users access to the file location and the information is available for them to download.

Communication

The internet has become a communication tool that allows users to use an internet connection and webcams on both users' computers to do a face-to-face video chat using applications such as Skype or Facetime.

With the development of VoIP, internet users can make telephone calls using a data connection instead of a telephone connection. The initial set up costs of a VOIP service are generally high as special telephones are needed to make the data calls. However, after the equipment has been bought, the call costs are significantly lower than landline calls. These services can then also be used for telephone conferences or video conferences.

Another firm favourite among internet users is text messaging using applications such as Facebook Messenger and WhatsApp. This costs much less than sending a message using a Short Message Service (SMS) as the user is only charged for the data that is used.

Power break 2.7   INDIVIDUAL WORK

Your manager has received a very high telephone bill. At closer inspection, he realises that the call costs keep increasing. As the secretary, you are instructed to do research on VoIP and text messaging as a cheaper alternative to telephone calls.

WHAT DO WE KNOW AND WHERE TO NEXT?

This module covered the concept of office automation. We named the principles it is based on and the effects it has on the secretary/management assistant. We also considered how technological developments have contributed to office automation and how these changes made the integration of electronic equipment possible.

Unit 2.2 examined the impact of the microcomputer on the customer and the wider community. We then moved on to the ergonomics of the electronic office and what its implications are on aspects such as human resource requirements, communication links, temperature control and lighting. We covered its effects on office layout, desktop arrangement and work routine.

Unit 2.4 considered the features of electronic appointment scheduling and the benefits of electronic diaries. Later, we discussed electronic document storage and retrieval in the paper-less office, the advantages and disadvantages of electronic document storage, coding and labelling electronically stored document, and we compared electronic filing and indexing systems to traditional filing and indexing systems. The module concluded with discussions on electronic mail (email) and the internet.

The next module covers advanced secretarial functions.

Revisiting the learning objectives

Now that you have completed this module you should have achieved the learning objectives listed in the table below.

Learning objective	What you have learned	✔
Define the concept office automation, name the principles it is based on and briefly explain its effect on the secretary/management assistant.	Office automation is the process of moving from a manual system of doing tasks to using an automatic solution for repetitive office tasks such as document filing. It has the benefit of helping the secretary get through more tasks in a shorter time.	☐
Briefly explain how technological developments (hardware, software, digital systems, and data links) have contributed to office automation and how these have made the integration of electronic equipment possible.	Office automation has grown exponentially because of faster, smaller and more powerful hardware, software, digital systems and data links. Electronic equipment such as scanners and, all-in-one printers have become an integrated part of the electronic office.	☐
List the applications of computer technology in the business world and elucidate the impact on the lives of the customers.	In the business world, computers perform tasks, such as communication, creating spreadsheets, creating documents, and electronic document storage and retrieval. Customers gain benefits such online ordering and electronic account payment.	☐

continued on next page …

Learning objective	What you have learned	✔
List the applications of microcomputers in the wider community and particularly in business enterprises and briefly elucidate the impact on the lives of office workers in general and secretaries/management assistants in particular.	The wider community also benefit from the business world using computers in the many ways, including: • online submission of tax returns • advertising and filling of vacant positions • obtaining bursaries or applying for funding.	☐
Briefly elucidate on the ergonomics of the electronic office.	Ergonomics in the electronic office is aimed at ensuring that the office worker has the ideal work environment to work most productively.	☐
List and briefly explain the basic elements of the electronic office and the implications of office automation.	In the electronic office, there is a greater reliance on computers and technology to perform routine repetitive tasks making the office workers more productive.	☐
Explain how office automation effects office layout, desktop arrangements, work routine (in the office, working away from office, accessing information nationally and internationally), and list the positive and negative effect it has on office workers.	Office automation has improved office layout by reducing the need for bulky cabinets to store reams and reams of paper. The workers' desktops are more organised with much less clutter from piles of paper.	☐
Briefly explain the key features of an electronic diary and list the points to consider in choosing an appropriate electronic appointment-scheduling program.	The electronic diary is used to schedule events, appointments and allows the user to be reminded of key appointments. The choice of electronic diary is dependent on compatibility with different platforms such as desktop computer, tablet computer and cellphone.	☐
Briefly explain on the advantages of an electronic diary compared to the traditional diary.	Electronic diaries allow users to make changes to appointments and will automatically update all affected persons.	☐
Briefly explain the concept of 'the paper-less office/electronic office' and point out how it differs from the traditional filing system.	The paper-less office/electronic office requires much less space than the traditional office. It is more flexible, durable and more secure.	☐
Compare the different media for electronic document/data storage (diskettes, hard disk, network server, CD Rom, magnetic tapes, etc.), explain on the advantages and disadvantages thereof and motivate the use of back-up copies.	The different storage media, such as diskettes, hard drives, network server, CD ROM, magnetic tape, USB flash drive and cloud storage, each have benefits that are similar in nature.	☐
Explain the coding and labelling of diskettes and, given a case study on types of information to be stored on diskettes, propose the proper coding and labelling for such information.	When coding and labelling diskettes, the organisation can use either alphabetical, numeric or an alphanumeric system.	☐

continued on next page ...

Learning objective	What you have learned	✔
Propose an effective filing system for diskettes in diskette holders/storage boxes.	When filing diskettes in a diskette holder it is recommended to use dividers that are labelled based on the organisation's preferred indexing system.	☐
Compare an electronic and traditional filing index system regarding accessibility, time to look up index, speed of recovery/retrieval and updating.	Electronic filing and indexing systems are office space savers with easier retrieval and retention of information but may result in job losses for workers. Traditional filing and indexing systems are suitable for all businesses but lack flexibility and ease of access to information.	☐
Briefly explain the concepts of computeroutput-microfilm (COM) and computerassisted retrieval (CAR) as methods of electronic documents storage and retrieval linked to a microform system.	Computer-output-microfilm converts electronic documents (data) onto microfilm to archive documents. Computer assisted retrieval is a document and retrieval system that uses computerised indexing, bar coding and reading technologies to help with document storage and retrieval.	☐
Define the concept of electronic mail (email) and explain the following in this connection: communication devices, data links, protocol, applications/ uses of email, advantages and disadvantages and forms of email.	Email is the most commonly used means of communication in the business world. Communication devices can send and receive information over digital or analogue technologies such as fibre routers, WiFi routers, modems and LTE routers. Email protocol such as IMAP, POP3 or SMTP determine how emails are stored, retrieved and sent. The advantages of email include sending information electronically globally, but a disadvantage is that IMAP email storage is limited by the email service provider.	☐
Define the concept internet and explain the following forms of internet uses: World Wide Web, electronic mail, Voice over Internet Protocol (VoIP), file sharing, streaming media, webcams, social interaction and cloud computing.	The internet or World Wide Web is platform that allows users to gain access to information stored in a shared database. Its uses include communication (email, text), entertainment (video, music or television), social interaction (Facebook, Twitter, Instagram). Webcams uses include video communication between two or more people. Cloud computing allows users to store and retrieve information in storage that is available on the internet server of a cloud computing service provider.	☐

Assessment

1. Multiple choice

Choose the correct answer from the various options provided. Choose only A, B, C or D and write it next to the question number.

1.1 A/An _____ accepts output data for processing and converts it into usable form.

    A processor

    B output device

    C storage device

    D input device

1.2 A _____ contains reference data which is normally altered/updated infrequently and transaction data which is built up over time.

    A a transaction file

    B a master file

    C a reference file

    D database

1.3 _____ is the integration of a range of electronic devices into a total support system to serve the needs of the office.

    A Routine processing

    B Staff development

    C Office automation

    D Office development

1.4 The most commonly used method of communication today is _____

    A email

    B Facebook

    C Twitter

    D SMS

1.5 If someone sends an email to the business email address and an automatic reply goes to the sender. This is called _____ .

    A Voice over Internet Protocol

    B email autoresponder

    C Post Office Protocol

    D Simple Message Transfer Protocol

$(5 \times 1 = 5)$

[5]

2. True or false

Choose whether the following statements are true or false. Write down the number of the question and 'true' or 'false'.

2.1 Transmitting graphics is one of the advantages of electronic mail.

2.2 A web page has several websites linked to it.

2.3 Electronic diaries can provide users with timely reminders of upcoming events, appointments or tasks.

2.4 Streamlining is one of the principles of automation.

2.5 An SD card can be used to as a backup storage media for a personal computer.

$(5 \times 1 = 5)$

[5]

3. Match the columns

Choose a description from Column B that matches the word/item in Column A. Write only the letter (A–E) next to the question number.

Column A	Column B
3.1 Hardware	A. Google Chrome
3.2 Data links	B. set of procedures that apply when communicating
3.3 Work routine	C. laptop computer
3.4 Protocol	D. links used in telecommunications to share information
3.5 Software	E. steps followed to achieve a specific task

$(5 \times 2 = 10)$

[10]

4. Short questions

4.1 List four principles of office automation. $(4 \times 1 = 4)$

4.2 List five tasks a microcomputer performs in the business world. $(5 \times 1 = 5)$

4.3 Identify six benefits customers gain from businesses using microcomputers. $(6 \times 1 = 6)$

4.4 List five implications of office automation. $(5 \times 1 = 5)$

4.5 List five points to consider in choosing an appropriate electronic appointment scheduler. $(5 \times 1 = 5)$

4.6 List five benefits of the internet. $(5 \times 1 = 5)$

[30]

5. Long questions

5.1 Electronic mail is most commonly used mode of communication in the business world. Discuss five advantages of electronic mail (email). $(5 \times 2 = 10)$

5.2 Name six disadvantages of social networks. $(6 \times 1 = 6)$

5.3 Discuss how the following technological advancements in the following items have changed office automation:

    5.3.1 hardware

    5.3.2 software

    5.3.3 digital systems

    5.3.4 data links $(4 \times 3 = 12)$

5.4 Explain five impacts that microcomputers have had on the lives of office workers and secretaries/management assistants. $(5 \times 2 = 10)$

5.5 Provide three advantages and three disadvantages of email. $(6 \times 2 = 12)$

[50]

Grand total: 100 marks

ADVANCED SECRETARIAL FUNCTIONS

This module considers the following aspects of advanced secretarial functions:

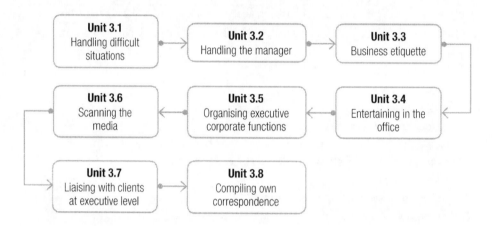

Learning objectives

After completing this module, you should be able to do the following:

- Recommend and motivate the best possible action to take to deal with difficult situations in the office including sexual harassment, gossip, complaints, criticism, unfair pressure, disrespect of access control, breach of confidentiality, etc. by clients, supervisors or colleagues.
- Compile guidelines for secretaries/management assistants with reference to the following: working for more than one manager, working in a team, problem solving, decision making, art of listening and assertiveness.
- Explain the secretary's/management assistant's role of gatekeeper to protect the manager.
- Be able to handle various difficult situations relating to the manager.
- Compile a set of guidelines for business etiquette, protocol and official protocol for secretaries/management assistants.
- Explain the guidelines for entertaining in the office and in a simulated situation, correctly demonstrate the skills of office entertaining by serving tea and refreshments to invited guests.

continued on next page …

Learning objectives

- Explain the procedure to be followed by a secretary/management assistant when organising executive corporate functions.
- Briefly explain why it is necessary for a secretary/management assistant to scan the media.
- Design a system for storing and indexing useful information obtained from scanning the media, including a list of contact persons and/or business enterprises and follow-up action to be taken.
- Explain in detail the general business policy on and prescriptions to be followed by a secretary/management assistant when liaising with clients at executive level.
- Compile a list of guidelines for secretaries/management assistants for compiling own correspondence (including the use of the corporate identity).

Key terms

acronym	harassment	tactful
confidentiality	induction programme	VIP
corporate identity	letterhead	weightings
etiquette	proofread	
gatekeeper	salutation	

Starting point

Verushna has gained significant understanding of her role as secretary but Roland wants her now to look at more advanced secretarial functions. He explains to Verushna that this module will help to equip her with the necessary skills and knowledge needed for advanced secretarial functions.

There are many challenges that you will face as a secretary/management assistant and being able to professionally deal with each activity will prove to your manager(s) that you can provide work of a high standard. When your manager expects you to be able to deal with complex tasks of organising corporate functions or entertaining in the office, you need to show that you have the necessary skills and knowledge to make it a success. When you work with multiple managers or even an incompetent manager, understanding business etiquette, protocol will be common place for you as an executive secretary. Let's join Verushna in getting better insights into advanced secretarial functions.

Figure 3.1 A successful secretarial career can be fulfilling.

UNIT 3.1 Handling difficult situations

The workplace, like any environment where people are actively participating, leads to positive and negative experiences. We all have enough positive life experience, but we also need to be prepared for negative life experiences or difficult situations that we need to deal with. As a secretary, how you deal with these difficult situations will help to improve as a person and can enhance the reputation of the manager and/or organisation, at the same time:

3.1.1 Difficult situations in the office

This section considers how to handle some of the difficult situations that may occur in an office environment.

Sexual harassment

This section discusses sexual harassment in the workplace. You will see how to deal with any unwanted sexual **harassment** and shows what you could do if you are the victim of sexual harassment.

What is sexual harassment?
Sexual harassment includes:

Figure 3.2 Sexual harassment can include unwanted physical contact or sexual advances.

* unwanted physical contact
* sexual advances
* verbal harassment, especially inappropriate sexual comments
* unwelcome gestures or whistling
* comments about a person's body
* indecent exposure
* continual enquiries about a person's sex life
* having to do a strip search by or in the presence of a member of the opposite sex
* unwelcome display of sexual pictures and/or sexual objects
* sexual assault
* where a person in authority like a manager, supervisor or co-worker asks for sexual favours in exchange for promotions, bonuses, salary increases, etc.
* rape.

DEFINITION

harassment – aggressive pressure or intimidation

Sexual harassment can occur in front of witnesses or it could happen privately. To be able to take proper action against someone accused of sexual harassment, the victim will need to supply evidence of the incident.

How to deal with sexual harassment in the workplace?

All organisations should have a policy that defines sexual harassment and details the consequences of violations of the policy. In addition, all employees in the organisation must be educated on what sexual harassment is and what the consequences are if it occurs in the workplace.

You should try to:

- maintain a safe distance from members of the opposite sex
- avoid playing or flirting in the office
- avoid temptations
- avoid compliments
- address the ladies as Miss or use first names
- avoid using nicknames
- avoid physical contact that could be misunderstood by someone as flirting.

Figure 3.3 Avoid sexual harassment by maintaining a polite distance from people of the opposite sex.

What can you do if sexual harassment has occurred?

If sexual harassment has occurred, the following action should be taken:

- The victim should report it to management and/or the human resources department immediately.
- The victim should provide as many details as possible, including the names of any witnesses of the act.
- The manager and/or human resources should make the services of a counsellor available to help the victim to deal with this experience.

- The manager and/or human resources should investigate the allegations and obtain statements from the victim, the perpetrator(s) and any witnesses. A case file should be opened to keep a record of the investigation.
- If the allegations are proven as truthful, the line manager/human resources should recommend any corrective actions to be taken against the perpetrator(s). This can include a reprimand, a verbal warning, a written warning, suspension, dismissal and/or criminal prosecution.
- Where the allegations cannot be proven, a record should be kept of the allegation and the result of the investigation.
- If the case warrants criminal prosecution, all evidence and notes on the incident should be handed over to the police for further investigation.

> **Did you know?** The #MeToo movement is an international movement against sexual harassment and assault. #MeToo spread in 2017 as a hashtag used on social media to help bring to the fore the widespread and frequent occurrences of sexual assault and harassment, especially in the workplace. The movement followed soon after public revelations of sexual misconduct allegations against former American movie director Harvey Weinstein.

Figure 3.4 The #MeToo movement has become a worldwide phenomenon.

Gossip

Gossip is casually talking about someone else on matters that are personal and cannot be confirmed as true. Gossip is something that should be avoided at all costs as it can hurt the person who is the subject of discussion. The best way to deal with gossip is to stop it before it goes too far. As soon as someone says, 'Did you hear about so and so …?', politely reply that it is none of your business and that you would rather not like to know the details.

Figure 3.5 Gossip can hurt a person.

If the person spreading the stories is persistent, make it clear that if they do not stop then you will have to report the matter to your manager, human resources and/or the person they are talking about.

Complaints

A complaint is an outward expression of a dislike for something or someone. Complaints can be seen as an opportunity to improve a process or a behaviour. For example, if a customer calls in and has a complaint about a product, you, as a secretary/management assistant, should tell the manager about the complaint. The manager can then assess if the complaint is justified and take the necessary steps to make changes to the product or service. Say, for instance, a customer calls to complain that the cellphone bought from the company keeps switching off for no reason. As there could be many causes of this problem, the manager should first try to get more information about the complaint, and if necessary, take up the matter with the company research and development team.

Aggression

Aggression is a feeling of anger that leads to violence. It is behaviour that suggests or indicates total disregard for the rights, feelings, needs, opinions and beliefs of others.

Aggression in the workplace could lead to someone getting physically hurt or result in a hostage situation. If you are the victim of aggression:

- remain calm and keep talking calmly to the aggressor
- listen to what the aggressor has to say and do not dismiss their issue(s) as unimportant
- make sure that the aggressor cannot harm anyone; this will require them to trust the person that they are dealing with.

If necessary, you can ensure that the aggressor is handled by a trained professional, such as a hostage negotiator, a psychologist or a trained counsellor. If the aggressor has made any demands, keep reminding them that if they want their demands met, they must not harm anyone.

Finally, do not try to take the law into your own hands, even if you have been trained in physical combat. This may result in you and others getting hurt.

Criticism

Criticism is an expression of a dislike of someone or something based on apparent faults or mistakes. Positive criticism helps to make a person improve their behaviour or increase productivity, whereas negative criticism can lead to the person being hurt and/or a decrease in productivity.

Unfair pressure

Unfair pressure or peer pressure is when someone is forced into doing something that is against their will because everyone else is doing it, for example, if at an office party someone is forced to drink alcohol because everyone at the party is drinking. To avoid unfair pressure, you should remain assertive and to stick to your own principles and not allow the pressure to get to you.

Disrespect of access control

Disrespect of access control happens when someone does not want to follow the rules when entering the workplace, for example, if all workers need to clock in when they arrive at work and someone just refuses to clock in. All protocol, including the rules that apply at access controls, must be clearly explained to new employees when they join the company. Other employees should be regularly reminded of these access control rules.

Breach of confidentiality

Breach of **confidentiality** is the unauthorised use of confidential information. This could harm the business and anyone who has access to confidential business information is under a legal obligation not to misuse it. As a secretary/management assistant, you would be required to deal with confidential information on a regular basis. You should report any breach of confidentiality to management as soon as possible so that management can assess how to deal with the offender. A breach of confidentiality can damage the

> **DEFINITION**
>
> **confidentiality** – the entrusted way to hold important information secretly

business or the manager/business' reputation and could lead to a disciplinary hearing against that person or someone being fired.

3.1.2 Guidelines for secretaries/management assistants

This section gives some workplace guidelines for secretaries/management assistants.

Working for more than one manager

Flashback to N4: Module 1 of *Office Practice* N4 discussed working for more than one manager and the importance and aim of teamwork in business. Go back and re-read the section to refresh your memory.

When working for more than one manager, you, as a secretary/management assistant, should keep the following in mind:

- Each manager has their own personality and way of working. Some managers require attention to detail, while others will be more lenient and overlook small mistakes.
- You should remain impartial when dealing with the managers and should not be seen to favour one manager's work over another. However, there will be times when work must be done urgently. In these circumstances, the manager should agree with the other managers that the task is urgent and that it is an exceptional situation.

Figure 3.6 A secretary should remain impartial when dealing with more than one manager.

- You will have to deal with multiple diaries and should coordinate efforts wherever possible. For example, if both managers need to attend a regional conference, it would be better to make the flight, hotel and shuttle bookings all at once as opposed to doing them separately.
- When your goals are set it is important to note whether there are different **weightings** applied to different managers. This will determine whether you should give more time and effort to tasks for a certain manager or whether you should treat all managers equally.
- There could be scenarios where you will have to stand in for someone who is off sick or on leave. In this situation, the managers need to agree on and inform you of the priorities and the way you should work.
- You should remain in constant contact with both managers to update them on progress on tasks each has requested. Keep notes of the discussions to ensure that they have been clearly understood and that the work is completed by the expected due date.

Working in a team

The principles of good teamwork include the following:
- There should be a common goal or objective that the team wants to achieve.
- Working in a team provides work colleagues an opportunity to mix with each other.
- Each team member should have a role, with the related responsibilities clearly identified.
- The team should communicate regularly, with each team member accountable for their tasks within the team.
- The team members should trust each other to complete their respective activities in time.
- The team should evaluate progress to ensure that they can meet their objectives/goals.
- Team members are all unique and will each add a different perspective to the team. For example, someone may be a good communicator but may need a technical person to assist in preparing a proper presentation. Where the team member's skills complement each other, it could help the team to be more successful.

Figure 3.7 Team members are all unique and will each add a different perspective to the team.

DEFINITION

weightings – applying different levels of importance to something

---

- The team should have a team leader to help plan and run team meetings, check the team's progress, and talk on behalf of the team.
- The team leader should make sure that all team members actively participate in discussions and that everyone feels that they are important in the team.
- The team should agree on a process to make effective decisions. It could be that decisions are made by most of the team members agreeing on an action, or it could be left to the team leader to make the final decision on what action to take.
- The team should celebrate successes and work on overcoming problem areas.

The advantages of teamwork include the following:
- There is increased efficiency in a team, especially when team members motivate each other.
- Teamwork provides the ability to focus different minds on the same problem.
- Teamwork provides team members with a support structure that can help them to be more productive.
- Better ideas can be generated in a team.
- Team members can feel a greater sense of accomplishment reaching a team target as opposed to reaching an individual target.
- Working as part of a team enables more people to be part of the decision-making process and they will feel like they were included in the final decision.
- Teamwork helps to develop team members' skills as team members can learn from each other.
- Teamwork encourages the development of networks that can be used in the future.
- Teamwork can help a team member deal with setbacks and provide different approaches to solving the problem.

Problem solving

Problem solving is an important aspect in any business environment. As previously discussed, each team member brings a different skill set to the team. The team leader must help the team members to bring these unique individual skills to the fore to help in a problem-solving situation.

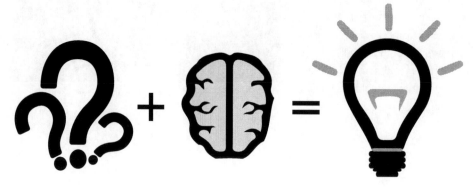

Figure 3.8 Problem solving is an important part of any business environment.

These are the steps to follow in an effective problem-solving process:

1. Identify the problem.

   Use the 5 W's and 1 H approach:
   - What?
   - Where?
   - When?
   - Why?
   - Who?
   - How?

2. Find alternative solutions to solve the problem.

   Use different approaches to find a possible solution, such as:
   - brainstorming (finding random solutions to the problem)
   - consult experts (for example, consult a lawyer if there is a legal issue that needs to be resolved)
   - field force analysis (identify the problem, identify the solution and map the difference)
   - scenario manager (use different scenarios and try them as a possible solution. In this way, you can identify the worst- and best-case scenarios).

3. Evaluate each alternative to see which option is viable.
4. Select the most appropriate solution.
5. Apply the solution to solve the problem.
6. Re-assess to see if the solution has solved the problem.
7. If unsuccessful, retry with another solution.

If successful, celebrate the success achieved!

Decision making

To be able to make the most effective decision, all relevant information should be available. As indicated in the previous section on problem solving, the team must evaluate various alternatives and decide which option is the best solution. Here are the seven steps in the decision-making process:

1. Identify the decision.
2. Gather information.
3. Identify alternatives.
4. Weigh the evidence.
5. Choose among the alternatives.
6. Take appropriate action.
7. Review the decision taken.

The art of listening

The art of listening is very important as managers will often just give verbal instructions and the secretary/management assistant is expected to execute the verbal instruction.

Figure 3.9 It is important to listen properly in any business encounter.

Listening is divided into different categories, namely:
- passive listening
- active listening
- critical listening
- appreciative listening
- empathetic listening.

Passive listening
Passive listening is when we listen but do not provide any form of feedback to acknowledge that we understand the message.

Active listening
Active listening is when we listen and acknowledge that we understand the message. Active listening is about focusing on the message and not being distracted by any noise or disturbance.

Critical listening
Critical listening involves some sort of problem solving. When we listen critically, we will try to evaluate the advantages and disadvantages of the problem. Critical listeners will try to be objective and decide upon the facts, and not allow the speaker to influence them.

Appreciative listening
Appreciative listening is about first understanding what is being said before responding to it. If necessary, the listener can ask questions in a non-threatening way. When we listen for appreciation, we are ultimately listening for pleasure, for example, at a music concert or a social event.

Empathetic listening

Empathetic listening is when we listen with empathy to someone who is unhappy or dissatisfied with something. Empathetic listeners give verbal and non-verbal cues that show that they are listening and provide comfort and advice.

Assertiveness

Assertiveness is standing up for what is your rights and openly and honestly expressing your thoughts, feelings and beliefs. It is done without aggression, threats, demands or treading on the rights, feelings, needs and opinions of others. Assertiveness is about addressing the issue without offending the person. It is finding a win-win in the relationship.

For example, if someone shouts at you for no apparent reason, you could say, 'When you shout at me it makes me feel insecure and I would appreciate it if you rather speak to me calmly, so we can make progress in our relationship.'

You can be assertive in the workplace by:

- being constructive in making decisions
- saying 'no' to an unreasonable request from someone
- having a different (but valid) opinion than others at a meeting
- having the ability to handle different personalities of customers and their needs
- having the ability to handle customers' queries with tact and respect
- being firm in your decisions, with a warm friendly smile.

Figure 3.10 Believe in yourself and stand up for your rights.

Power break 3.1 INDIVIDUAL WORK

How would you resolve the following scenarios in the workplace?

Scenario	Solution
1. Sexual harassment Your colleague is continually enquiring about your sex life.	
2. Gossip Your co-workers are saying negative things about your boss to you.	
3. Aggression A co-worker is using aggressive statements which embarrass others.	
4. Breach of confidentiality During a work function, you overheard one of your colleagues discussing the terms of a new contract with a visitor.	

UNIT 3.2 Handling the manager

This unit explores the role of the secretary as a **gatekeeper** for the business and gives some suggestions of how to deal with an incompetent manager.

3.2.1 The role of the secretary as gatekeeper

As a secretary/management assistant, you may also be responsible for the reception and switchboard duties in the office environment. As such, you play an important role in controlling access to the manager(s).

As the gatekeeper, you must screen all visitors arriving at the office. Confirm if they have an appointment and contact the person that they would like to meet. Let the visitor be seated while you contact the person they are visiting. Ensure that the visitor does not wander off in the building unattended.

You must also screen all incoming calls. Greet the caller by giving the name of the business and your name, and by saying ' 'How may I assist you?'

During the call:
- listen attentively to the caller and make short hand notes
- find out the reason for the call and make a note of it
- keep the caller on the line while transferring the call to the person they requested.

When you transfer the call to someone, say who is on the line and the reason for their call. If the person is unavailable to take the call, take a message.

> **DEFINITION**
>
> **gatekeeper –** a person who controls access to a business

3.2.2 Dealing with an incompetent manager

As the secretary/management assistant, you should try to understand all aspects of your manager(s), and all their strengths and weaknesses. When you notice that a manager has a weakness in a certain area you need to be **tactful** in ensuring that the this weakness does not result in the business suffering.

The following sections will help you to deal with a manager's failures in certain areas.

Set priorities

To be effective in the business, you must set clear priorities. If the manager has not set clear priorities for the work given to you, you need to ask the following:
* How urgent is the task?
* How important is the task?

Figure 3.11 To be effective in the business, you must set clear priorities.

Something that is both important and urgent requires immediate action. For example, if someone suffers a heart attack at the reception, it is important and urgent as someone's life is dependent on our actions and the person may die if our actions are not quick enough.

However, there are things that are not important and not urgent. For example, when a friend arrives at your desk to talk about last night's soccer match or about a friend's birthday party, this is neither important nor urgent.

> **DEFINITION**
>
> **tactful** – dealing sensitively with others or with difficult issues

Table 3.1 gives the priority level for some different work scenarios.

Table 3.1 Levels of priority

Important, not urgent	Urgent, important
Planning Budgeting Savings Research Setting goals and objectives Studying Exercise Writing a book	Crisis Heart attack Fire Armed robbery Hijacking Panic attack Cramming for an exam Missing a flight
Not important, not urgent	**Urgent, not important**
Social visit by a friend Gossip Watching television Chatting on your phone Surfing the internet	Telephone ringing Knock at the door Messenger arriving with a parcel Someone calling your name

Return messages

If your manager does not return messages, you could do the following:

- Screen all incoming calls to identify only important calls that the manager needs to attend to.
- Send the manager an email message with the details of any important call/visitor that needs to be attended to.
- Find out whether the manager received the message.
- Check your manager's calendar to make sure that there is a time available to attend to messages. If the calendar is crowded, schedule a daily time slot for the manager to attend to the messages.
- Follow up later with the person who called to confirm that your manager has returned the call. If not, then apologise on behalf of your manager and tell the caller that you will remind the manager of the call as soon as possible.
- If the call is urgent, you could call the person and immediately transfer the call to the manager.

Meet promises

If you find yourself in a situation where your manager has not kept promises, you could:

- place a reminder on any emails in which the manager has promised to do something
- assess what needs to be done and get all the information your manager may need to meet the promise
- remind your manager at least a day or two before the due date of any promises that need to be fulfilled.

If your manager has made a promise that you feel will be very difficult to keep, make your manager aware of the challenges that the promise will create for the rest of the work schedule.

Convey expectations

Managers should make time, especially with new staff, to discuss what the staff are expected to do. If your manager does not do this, you could help by doing the following:

- Keep a record of when a new employee is scheduled to start work.
- Obtain a copy of the new employee's job description and keep this on file for the manager.
- Create a draft **induction programme** for the new employee so that the manager has this ready for any discussions.
- Schedule an appointment in the manager's diary to discuss job requirements with the new employee.
- Confirm whether the manager has had a chance to look at the job description and induction programme of the new employee before the person arrives.

Criticism or praise of the secretary's/management assistant's work

A manager should give regular feedback (or criticism) to the secretary/management assistant on how work performance has been. If the manager fails to do this, you could help by scheduling a quarterly performance review meeting with the manager to discuss:

- the targets for the year
- the progress made towards achieving the targets set for the previous period
- successes in the past quarter
- areas of improvement identified
- training requirements.

As the secretary/management assistant, you could also have regular meetings with your manager to review ongoing work and ask for honest feedback.

To deal with criticism, be assertive and tell the manager how you feel when the criticism is given. Say how you would prefer the criticism to be positive so that it can help you to grow as a person.

Clear and effective communication

Effective communication is when the message that is received is the same as the message that was sent. If you find that your manager does not communicate clearly, you could do the following:

> **DEFINITION**
>
> **induction programme** – the process used within many businesses to welcome new employees to the company and prepare them for their new role

- At the start of the day, meet with the manager to discuss what needs to be completed on that day. You could also discuss progress on existing tasks and provide reminders of upcoming events and tasks.

Figure 3.12 Try to have regular morning meetings with your manager to discuss the work schedule.

- Be assertive when communicating with the manager so that the communication remains positive.
- Make notes during discussions with the manager and review these during the day/ week to see what has been completed or what requires support to complete.
- If the manager is not a talkative person, try to encourage the manager to talk about the work and pass on the correct information so that everyone knows exactly what must be done.

Be consistent

A consistent manager will make the same decision under different circumstances. Consistency comes from following the same process to reach the right decision. Say, for instance, there is a customer complaint about a product. If there is a record of previous complaints, you could remind the manager of what decisions were taken and help the manager to make the right decision.

Locating the manager

You should always be aware of the manager's movements during the work day. You can achieve this by doing the following:

- Keep the manager's diary up-to-date.
- Screen the manager's calls to identify any potential meetings that may arise during the day.

- Be aware of any personal commitments that have been made that require the manager to be unavailable during the day.
- If necessary, contact the manager on a cellphone/home phone number or other contact number to establish the manager's whereabouts.

Case study

Mr Sloppy Joe is the manager of Global Investments in Port Elizabeth and he has been transferred to the post of regional manager based in the Cape Town branch. You are the secretary in the Port Elizabeth branch and your colleague, Sheila Snow has contacted you as she will be Mr Joe's new secretary in Cape Town. Sheila has had some problems concerning Mr Joe's management style and she would like to know how you dealt with him regarding his failure to:

- set priorities
- return messages
- meet promises
- convey expectations
- praise the secretary's/management assistant's work
- communicate clearly
- be consistent
- inform the secretary/management assistant of his/her whereabouts or time of return.

Power break 3.2   INDIVIDUAL WORK

On your own, make a list of all the tasks you must complete for the week. Place two activities in each of the sections of the table below.

Important, not urgent	Urgent, important
Not important, not urgent	Urgent, not important

UNIT 3.3 **Business etiquette**

All organisations have a culture or way of working that makes them an active part of civil society. The organisation will share their way of doing business with their employees – this is part of the business **etiquette** associated with the organisation. Business etiquette strives to establish a positive and uplifting work environment for all employees and shows civil society the positive side of the organisation.

Business etiquette starts from the personality and character of the leadership in the organisation. The leadership will set out general business principles that they want within the organisation and formulate a code of conduct for employees to help live up to these business principles.

3.3.1 Business principles

Table 3.2 gives some examples of business principles that an organisation can put in place.

Table 3.2 Some business principles that an organisation can put in place

Principle	Description
Openness	The organisation does not hide information from employees or the public.
Honesty	The organisation is honest about its products, services and standards.
Integrity	The organisation applies the same standards across all departments and regions where it operates.
Delivering on promises	Society can rely on the organisation to deliver on the promises that it has made.
Quality	The organisation's products and/or services are associated with quality and will last for the expected life time of the product/service.

3.3.2 Protocol

As important as business etiquette is, so too is ensuring all employees follow the right protocols for business functions and events. For example, when introducing guests to management, ensure that all involved are able to easily identify the more senior people. Always introduce the junior person to the senior person. Protocol also dictates how a dinner, lunch or business breakfast will be arranged, for example, where the different guests are to be seated, the order in which tables will be served or that guests will line up for a buffet.

The State of the Nation address is a good example of how members of parliament and other instances follow protocol. The way that the soldiers, police and members of the

---

DEFINITION

etiquette – the correct conduct in a company/business, organisation or practice to render service and increase productivity

---

public line the streets and the order in which members of parliament enter the parliamentary buildings is done in a specific order. Similarly, there are set protocols when foreign heads of state are received in parliament. These protocols help to ensure that the guests are treated with the necessary dignity and respect.

3.3.3 Office protocol

Office protocol, in turn, is the rules of acceptable behaviour in the office, or good manners in an office. Office protocol includes doing the following:

- Greet your colleagues in the morning when you arrive at the office.
- Acknowledge an introduction with a smile.
- If asked to introduce a colleague, do so promptly and efficiently.
- Treat people like responsible adults.
- Treat others with respect. In this way you will earn their respect.
- Set a good example for your fellow colleagues.
- Be polite when talking to and dealing with your colleagues, customers, suppliers or others who you meet with during your day.
- Respect the rights, opinions, feelings, needs and beliefs of others.
- Do not attend to personal matters during office hours unless you have received approval from your supervisor to do so.
- Understand human needs and put yourself in the shoes of others.
- Do not use the organisation's assets for personal matters, for example, don't make copies of your personal documents on the photocopier.
- Use the organisation's name and titles policy or personal preference when addressing customer, colleagues and visitors.
- Be loyal to your colleagues by being honest and supporting each other in solving problems and avoiding gossip.
- Create a favourable working atmosphere for others.
- Keep your promises to others.
- Do not misuse your relationship with others to do your work for you.
- Show genuine interest in what others have to say in discussions.
- Maintain secrecy on anything that is not for public consumption.
- Help those who are in need and be considerate to others.
- Be assertive (but not overly assertive) in your communication with others.
- Make others aware of your whereabouts if you are not going to be at your workstation.
- Answer your colleagues' phones when they are not at their desk and give them the message(s) afterwards.
- Maintain proper personal hygiene in the office environment especially if you have a cold, flu or an upset stomach.
- Do not distract others while they are busy working.
- Knock when entering someone's office or a closed meeting room.
- Say goodbye to your colleagues when you leave the office.

UNIT 3.4 Entertaining in the office

There may be occasions where the organisation will host guests and either a meal or drinks will be served in the office environment. Entertaining in the office is different to entertaining at any other venue. Entertaining can vary from serving only tea/coffee to serving a light lunch or even having a social function such as a braai.

Figure 3.13 Entertaining in the office.

3.4.1 Guidelines for entertaining in the office

This section considers general guidelines to follow when entertaining in the office. We also discuss how to arrange tea/coffee and snacks for an office meeting.

General guidelines to follow when entertaining in the office

These are some general guidelines you could follow when entertaining in the office:

- Usually, the office is not suited for a full sit-down dinner/lunch but with some creativity it can be effectively used to entertain guests.
- Depending on the timing of the event, ensure that all staff are dressed appropriately to receive guests and to project the right image of the organisation.
- Ensure that the office has been cleaned and that any banners and decorations have been put in place well before the arrival of the guests.
- Ensure that all confidential documents have been secured/stored and that the office staffs' desks have been cleared before the guests arrive.
- Ensure that there is sufficient parking available for the guests and that there are signs posted along the way to guide them to the office.
- Management should talk to all staff before the event starts and give them an overview of what will happen and who is responsible for what activities. They should also ask the staff not to overindulge in the food or drinks and to make all guests feel welcome.
- Ensure that there is a welcoming committee to greet the guests (and perhaps offer welcome drinks) on their arrival.
- Have an attendance register for the guests to sign in.
- Give the guests an overview of the office layout. Point out where the toilets, emergency exits, and designated smoking areas are.
- Ensure that the public-address system is working and that the master of ceremonies makes guests aware of the programme for the function.
- If there is music, it should not be too loud.
- If alcohol is served, make sure that guests and staff do not over-indulge as this may give rise to unpleasant incidents in the office.

We now look at things to keep in mind when arranging an office meeting where tea/coffee and snacks are to be served.

Arranging tea and coffee for a meeting

When arranging for tea/coffee for a meeting, you (as secretary) should make sure you know what is needed. If you haven't already been told, you should ask your manager for the information and guidelines.

When arranging the event, you should know (or find out):

- the number of people who will be in the meeting.
- whether to include biscuits or sandwiches.
- whether the tea/coffee will be served in the meeting or at another venue, for example, in the staff kitchen or lounge area.
- the time the tea/coffee should be served.
- whether there are special dietary requirements, such as soy milk or artificial sweeteners.

You should serve the tea/coffee while it is still hot and provide enough crockery and cutlery for the number of people expected. Also make sure you place the coffee granules and tea bags in appropriate containers and do not serve them out of the normal packaging.

Arranging snacks for a meeting

Keep the following in mind when arranging snacks for a meeting:

- You (as secretary/management assistant) should know the caterer that provides the food and be confident that they maintain a high hygiene standard when preparing the food.
- Make sure that any special dietary food is properly labelled and kept separate from the other food.
- The food should be presentable when it is served, with contrasting colour garnishing. Parsley, lettuce, tomatoes and slices of lemon are usually used to improve the presentation of the food.
- If serving a hot meal, ensure that the meal is warm enough to eat when served.
- It is a good idea to include fruits and vegetables in a finger lunch.
- Provide crockery and utensils with the finger lunch so that people can dish up the food properly.

Power break 3.4   INDIVIDUAL WORK

Your manager has asked you to arrange the refreshments for a meeting at 12:00 where ten people will be in the company boardroom. Make a list of the activities that you need to consider when planning and preparing to serve the refreshments.

UNIT 3.5 **Organising executive corporate functions**

When organising executive corporate functions, you, as secretary/management assistant, should consider the following:

- Send invitations for the event out in good time to give the guests enough time to decide if they will attend the event. Include clear directions to the venue.
- If special guests (**VIPs**) have not responded by the RSVP (please reply) date, make a courteous follow-up call. This will show them that they are important to the organisation and may also prompt them to attend the event.

DEFINITION

VIP – Very Important Person

- When ordering the food, be aware of the dietary requirements of all the people who will be entertained. It may be necessary to rather order vegetarian meals to avoid meals not being acceptable because of religious reasons.
- Ensure that there is sufficient food and drinks for all the guests and staff.
- Carefully plan for the event and make sure that the key office staff are aware of the arrangements.
- It is a good idea to arrange name tags for all the staff and guests so that everyone knows who they are talking to during the event.
- Allocate a manager or senior staff member to look after a specific VIP.
- Ensure that protocol is followed when allocating guests to their tables. It is better if executives sit with management and the VIPs.
- Use place cards to indicate where each guest is to be seated. It is a clever idea to have a table layout at the entrance so that guests can easily find their allocated seating place when they arrive.
- If there is special seating for VIPs, have a staff member(s) guide them to their seats before any speeches are made.
- The menu should provide at least three courses (starter, mains and dessert) and should cater for all cultures.
- Menus should be placed on the tables so that the guests can see what will be served. The rest of the programme can be printed on the opposite side.

Power break 3.5 **PAIR WORK**

You and your colleague have been asked by your manager to draw up a checklist of items that you need to address to make the upcoming sales conference, which includes a corporate dinner, a huge success.

UNIT 3.6 **Scanning the media**

This unit turns to how the secretary/management assistant can help the organisation stay up-to-date with current events reported in the media. The media includes:
- television
- radio
- newspapers
- magazines
- social media
- websites.

3.6.1 Why is it necessary to scan the media?

It is necessary to scan the media to keep abreast with any developments that could impact on the organisation, its effectiveness and ultimate success.

Figure 3.14 A business needs to be aware of changes and developments in the business world.

3.6.2 Methods used to scan the media

A good way to keep abreast of development in the media is to subscribe to newsletters from newspapers, magazines or specific organisations. These online subscriptions will make it easier to obtain any updated information. Some subscriptions are free; for others, the company may have to pay a nominal amount per month or per annum.

The newsletters will be sent to the email address that was used to subscribe. The secretary will scan through the newsletter and identify items that affect the business. The secretary can then extract the important information and forward this information to the relevant person/department. Updates could relate to any of the following:

- new technology that has come onto the market
- new market entrants
- changes in legislation
- suppliers or customers in the news
- supply issues that could impact the organisation
- information on industrial action in certain business segments
- news about competitors
- new business opportunities
- tenders that have been advertised.

3.6.3 Storing and indexing information from media updates

You can store and index information as a soft copy or a printout copy kept in a file. For either, information can be indexed based on the following categories:

- Contact persons
- New business opportunities

- Tenders
- Supplier information
- Customer updates
- Technological changes
- Legal updates.

You can attach a note to a filed document giving any actions to be taken, as well as the name of the person responsible for the task.

Power break 3.6 INDIVIDUAL WORK

As a secretary/management assistant you need to be aware of what is currently happening outside the business environment that can impact on the business. Research two important aspects that could influence the business, in any of the following categories:

Research area	Impact on the business
1. Stock exchange prices	
2. Exports and imports	
3. Banking	
4. Government policies	
5. News (media)	
6. Political environment	

UNIT 3.7 **Liaising with clients at executive level**

All correspondence with clients at executive level should be closely scrutinised, especially by the secretary/management assistant. These are some procedures and checks that could be put in place:

- All correspondence should be done on an official company **letterhead** and reflect the organisation's information clearly including the business name, address, names of directors and contact numbers.
- The greetings and **salutations** on the correspondence must reflect the latest information for the recipient and should be addressed correctly, for example, Dear Mr Gumede.
- The subject line must summarise clearly what the correspondence is about.

DEFINITIONS

letterhead – the heading at the top of a sheet of paper; usually consists of the name and address of the business, logo or corporate design and sometimes a background image (watermark)

salutation – greeting normally used in written communication, for example, Dear Jane

- The first page of a report sent to executives should provide an executive summary of the full report.
- The tone of the correspondence should always be positive as you would like to retain or increase the customer's business.
- As the secretary/management assistant, avoid using slang, abbreviations and poor grammar in any correspondence.
- Check all correspondence for spelling and grammar before it is sent to the client.
- If the content is a legal document, ensure that the legal department or the company lawyer has reviewed and agreed to the document content before it is sent out.
- The manager must read through the draft document before giving consent to send it to the recipient(s).
- Make sure to present the printout copy in a neat, professional, and presentable layout.

Power break 3.7 **PAIR WORK**

Work in pairs in a role play. One student acts as a secretary/management assistant and the other as a client at executive level. The client needs assistance with something and the secretary/management assistant should provide the service.

1 Once the role play is completed, share with each other how you felt you were treated by the other.
2 Make recommendations on how to improve your treatment.

UNIT 3.8 **Compiling own correspondence**

As the secretary/management assistant, any correspondence that you send out to customers, suppliers, government organisations, and so forth, on the organisation's letterhead or with the corporate email signature represents the organisation.

3.8.1 Guidelines when compiling own correspondence

These are some guidelines to follow when you compile your own correspondence:
- All typing must be done neatly, without spelling and grammatical errors.
- As with correspondence to executives, if there is legal content in the correspondence, have the legal department or the company lawyer read through and agree to the content before it is sent out.
- For correspondence that your manager has dictated to you, have the manager **proofread** the content and sign it off before it is sent out.
- Your correspondence should be well structured and logical, with a start, a middle and an ending.

DEFINITION

proofread – to find and correct mistakes in text before it is printed or put online

- Write your correspondence in a manner that reflects your style and personality.
- Use everyday language and avoid using difficult words or phrases.
- Avoid using slang or unknown **acronyms** that could confuse the recipient of your correspondence.
- Your correspondence should be sincere, positive and non-offensive.
- Always read through your correspondence before printing it. You can make corrections on the electronic version of the document.
- Your correspondence should reflect positively on the corporate image of the organisation.

3.8.2 Corporate identity

When dealing with business forms, such as letterheads, invoices, delivery notes and catalogues, most organisations have a **corporate identity** that they would like reflected. As the secretary/management assistant, you play an important role in ensuring that the corporate identity is correctly reflected in all business forms that you use.

The corporate identity could consist of the following, or a combination of these:
- corporate colours
- design of the business forms
- design of the company logo
- slogans used in the company
- uniforms of the workers
- branded materials used for marketing the organisation (company T-shirt, company pen, etc.)

Power break 3.8   PAIR WORK

In pairs, research the corporate identity of your college. Look at the following aspects and answer the questions that follow:
- uniform
- slogan
- logo
- branded materials (T-shirts, pens, etc.).

1 What image does the corporate uniform create for the college?
2 Do the logo and slogan address the vision of the college?
3 Is the college's branded material an effective marketing tool? Motivate your answer.

DEFINITIONS

acronym – a word formed from the initial letters or groups of letters of words in a set phrase or series of words and pronounced as a separate word, such as OPEC for Organization of Petroleum Exporting Countries, or NATO for North Atlantic Treaty Organization

corporate identity – a lasting representation of how a firm views itself

WHAT DO WE KNOW AND WHERE TO NEXT?

This module considered how the secretary/management assistant handles difficult situations and deals with the manager. The module also covered business etiquette, the factors to consider when entertaining in the office and organising executive corporate functions. We also looked at why scanning the media is important and suggested some things to consider when liaising with clients at executive level. The module concluded by discussing the different aspects the secretary/management assistant must consider when compiling correspondence.

The next module discusses the economic environment. You will learn about human needs, consumer behaviour and the marketing of products. The module also covers the concept of market segregation, the types of business ownership and the need for and role of utility undertakings.

Revisiting the learning objectives

Now that you have completed this module you should have achieved the learning objectives listed in the table below.

Learning objective	What you have learned	✔
Recommend and motivate the best possible actions to take to deal with difficult situations in the office including sexual harassment, gossip, complaints, criticism, unfair pressure, disrespect of access control, breach of confidentiality, etc. by clients, supervisors or colleagues.	Sexual harassment is dealing with unwanted physical contact and other unacceptable behaviour. The company policy, education of staff and proper procedures to deal with those who contravene this policy is the best solution. Gossip should be stopped before it starts, complaints must be handled systematically. Criticism must be constructive to improve behaviour and productivity. Unfair pressure must be dealt with assertively, so too disrespecting access controls and breach of confidentiality.	☐
Compile guidelines for secretaries/management assistants with reference to the following: working for more than one manager, working in a team, problem solving, decision making, art of listening and assertiveness.	The secretary/management assistant working with more than one manager needs to agree with the manager on priorities and ways of working. Working in a team requires an understanding of what teamwork entails and what benefits it provides, such as problem solving and greater job satisfaction. Problem solving involves identifying the problem and finding an acceptable approach to overcome the problem. Decision making can be including input from all team members from just the team leader.	☐

continued on next page …

Learning objective	What you have learned	✔
	The art of listening includes: • passive listening • active listening • critical listening • appreciative listening • empathetic listening. Assertiveness is standing up for your rights, needs, feelings and opinions while still respecting the rights, needs, feelings and opinions of others.	
Explain the secretary's/management assistant's role of gatekeeper to protect the manager.	As a gatekeeper to the manager the secretary/management assistant helps to screen calls and visitors to ensure that the manager is not bothered by unimportant things.	☐
Be able to handle various difficult situations relating to the manager.	To deal with an incompetent manager, the secretary/management assistant should: • ensure that the manager sets priorities • help the manager to return messages • help the manager to meet promises • make it easier for the manager to give feedback on the work and provide constructive criticism • help the manager to be consistent by reminding the manager of previous experiences/actions taken. • devise a system to track the manager's whereabouts during the work day.	☐
Compile a set of guidelines for business etiquette, protocol and official protocol for secretaries/management assistants.	Business etiquette strives for a better working environment and improved productivity. Protocol is the set rules that must be followed to maintain order. Office protocol ensures right behaviour in the office environment.	☐
Explain the guidelines for entertaining in the office and in a simulated situation, correctly demonstrate the skills of office entertaining by serving tea and refreshments to invited guests.	Entertaining in the office requires the secretary/management assistant to organise the food and drinks and ensure that all protocols are followed. Tea/coffee and light snacks must be served as required by the manager.	☐
Explain the procedure to be followed by a secretary/management assistant when organising executive corporate functions.	When organising corporate functions, the secretary/management assistant should ensure that the invitations are sent out in time, guests are followed up on, VIPs are looked after by a senior person. The food, drinks, décor, crockery, cutlery are put out in the best possible way to show the guests that they are special.	☐
Briefly explain why it is necessary for a secretary/management assistant to scan the media.	To keep the business up-to-date with all the latest happenings in the business world, secretary/management assistant should scan online newsletters in the appropriate media and spread the relevant information to the business.	☐

continued on next page …

Learning objective	What you have learned	✔
Design a system for storing and indexing useful information obtained from scanning the media, including a list of contact persons and/or business enterprises and follow-up action to be taken.	The secretary/management assistant can store and index useful information in different categories, for example: • contact persons • new business opportunities • tenders • supplier information • customer updates • technological changes • legal updates.	☐
Explain in detail the general business policy on and prescriptions to be followed by a secretary/management assistant when liaising with clients at executive level.	When liaising with clients at executive levels, the secretary/management assistant must ensure that all documents are factually correct and do not expose the business from a legal point of view. The manager should read through and sign off the documents before it is sent to the clients.	☐
Compile a list of guidelines for secretaries/management assistants for compiling own correspondence (including the use of the corporate identity).	When sending off correspondence still requires the secretary/management assistant must communicate effectively and improve the corporate image of the business. The secretary/management assistant must ensure that the corporate identity and image of the business is enhanced by the proper use of business forms, uniforms, slogans, logos, etc.	☐

Assessment

1. Multiple choice

Choose the correct answer from the various options provided. Choose only A, B, C or D and write it next to the question number.

1.1 _____ is when people talk badly about the organisation.
  A   Gossip
  B   Advertising
  C   Praise
  D   Revelation

1.2 _____ is one of the guidelines of office etiquette.
  A   Selflessness
  B   Expectation
  C   Helpfulness/thoughtfulness
  D   Self-esteem

1.3 The most important thing to consider when formulating forms for the company is

_____ .
  A   the design of the form
  B   the introduction of the form
  C   the purpose of the form
  D   the application form

1.4 _____ is the way that professionals behave.
  A   Etiquette for professional people
  B   Guidelines for office etiquette
  C   Protocol
  D   Business etiquette

1.5 _____ provides people an opportunity to mix with each other.
  A   Isolation
  B   Teamwork
  C   Solitude
  D   Confinement

(5 × 1 = 5)

[5]

2. Match the columns

Choose a description from Column B that matches the word/item in Column A. Write only the letter (A–E) next to the question number.

Column A	Column B
2.1 Breach of confidentiality	A. The correct conduct of a company, organisation or practice to render service to increase productivity.
2.2 Aggression	B. The mixture of standing up for one's own rights without treading on the rights of others, expressing wishes, opinions and feelings directly and honestly.

continued on next page ...

Column A	Column B
2.3 Etiquette	C. The unauthorised divulging of confidential information.
2.4 Assertiveness	D. The polite manner of doing something in any situation
2.5 Protocol	E. Behaviour that disregards other people's rights, feelings and opinions.

$(5 \times 2 = 10)$

[10]

3. Short questions

Define the following terms:

3.1 sexual harassment (2)

3.2 confidentiality (2)

3.3 corporate identity (2)

3.4 letterhead (2)

3.5 VIP (2)

$(5 \times 2 = 10)$

[10]

4. Long questions

4.1 In your opinion, does sexual harassment happen to women only? Motivate your answer. $(2 \times 2 = 4)$

4.2 Give eight principles for women and men on how to avoid sexual harassment in the workplace. $(8 \times 2 = 16)$

4.3 Discuss nine important points a management assistant/secretary should keep in mind when doing work for two managers. $(9 \times 2 = 18)$

4.4 Name six situations in which being assertive at the workplace helps. $(6 \times 2 = 12)$

[50]

Grand total: 75 marks

THE ECONOMIC ENVIRONMENT

This module considers the following aspects of the electronic economic environment:

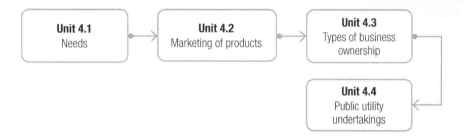

Unit 4.1
Needs

Unit 4.2
Marketing of products

Unit 4.3
Types of business ownership

Unit 4.4
Public utility undertakings

Learning objectives

After completing this module, you should be able to do the following:
- Explain human needs with reference to the following:
  - origin of needs
  - different types of needs (external and internal)
  - goals (things to satisfy needs)
  - the individual as a consumer.
- Briefly state how knowledge of human needs would affect a secretary's/management assistant's view of customers.
- Explain in detail the following determinants of consumer behaviour:
  - individual factors (needs and attitudes)
  - perception
  - learning ability
  - personality traits
  - the family
  - reference groups
  - income and standard of living.
- Briefly explain market segmentation, product positioning, different groups in the market and classification of consumer products.

continued on next page …

- Explain in detail the following aspects of a marketing strategy:
  - branding
  - packaging
  - pricing
  - distribution
  - advertising
  - promotions
  - product life cycle.
- Briefly explain the founding procedure for the following business enterprises:
  - sole proprietor
  - partnership
  - public company
  - private company
  - close corporation
  - informal.
- Explain the characteristics of the following business enterprises:
  - sole proprietor
  - partnership
  - public company
  - private company
  - close corporation
  - informal.
- Briefly explain why a secretary/management assistant has to have a basic knowledge of the types of business ownership.
- Briefly explain the need for and the role of utility undertakings (giving examples).

Key terms

creditor	monopoly	person
indigent	need	product life cycle
market	perception	

Starting point

Verushna's mentor has taught her that her role in the organisation requires her to have a sound knowledge of the economic environment in which the organisation operates. There are times when she will need to co-ordinate the invitations for new product launches or to be in contact with utility companies about the basic services needed for the organisation. Even understanding customer needs plays a key role in how she can support the management team. This all helps the organisation to keep pace with market trends and in some instances even becoming the market leader for certain products or services.

Figure 4.1 Verushna's mentor has shown her ways of keeping pace with market trends

UNIT 4.1 **Needs**

If I had to ask you to close your eyes and imagine a slice of freshly baked chocolate cake being drizzled with chocolate sauce and covered with your favourite fruit or nuts, what picture does this create in your mind? Does it create the desire to want to buy or bake a chocolate cake? This is how human beings are born – with a desire for certain things – and there are times that we will do anything to satisfy the desire or urge that we have.

4.1.1 Human needs

Several theories have been developed around human **needs**. Probably the most well-known is American psychologist Abraham Maslow's hierarchy of needs. Figure 4.2 illustrates the theory.

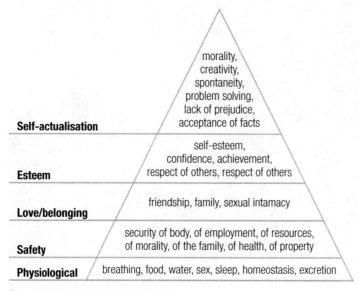

Figure 4.2 Maslow's hierarchy of needs

Maslow classified human needs into five categories:
1. Physiological needs
2. Safety needs
3. Love/belonging needs
4. Esteem needs
5. Self-actualisation needs.

> **DEFINITIONS**
>
> **need** – the desire or craving for something (goods or services) that gives us physical, social or psychological satisfaction
>
> **hierarchy** – a system in which people or things are arranged according to their importance

Physiological needs

Maslow believed that everyone has basic or primary needs that should form the base of our existence. This he termed, physiological needs and it included the need for breathing, food, water, housing, sleep, sex, etc.

Safety needs

At this level of human needs, Maslow included the need for security of employment, resources, family, health and physical protection. This level forms part of the primary human needs.

Love/belonging needs

Only when physiological and safety needs (primary needs) have been satisfied can we satisfy our social and other needs. At this level, our needs include the need for love, affection and companionship.

Esteem needs

The next level of needs involves what people think of themselves (their self-concept) and what others think of them (status and respect). This level includes the need for power, achievement, independence and self-confidence.

Self-actualisation needs

Self-actualisation needs refer to the need for personal development and the use of all our talents to become all that we are capable of becoming. Examples include being promoted to management, getting a sought-after qualification or writing a book, poem or a song.

Did you know? Human needs can also be classified as:
- natural needs (for example, light/water/fresh air)
- essential needs (for example, shelter/clothes/food)
- luxury needs (for example, telephones/cars/cellphones)
- need for protection (for example, protection against crime/terrorism)
- spiritual needs (for example, the need to worship/faith)
- cultural needs (for example, ethical/ecstasy/intelligence).

4.1.2 Satisfying customer needs

When a business has a product or a service that it would like to sell to willing buyers or consumers, the business needs to target that section or segment of the **market**. The business would use different marketing strategies to make the consumers aware of this product or service.

To be successful, a business should focus on understanding customer needs and working on products and/or services that customers are willing to pay for.

Table 4.1 shows the three categories of goods that satisfy needs.

Table 4.1 Categories of goods

Category of goods	Description
Consumer goods	Consumer goods are goods that are made to be consumed or used immediately to satisfy a need, for example, food, water/drinks and clothes.
Capital goods	Capital goods are goods that are used to produce consumer goods and other capital goods, for example, equipment and machinery.
Services	Services are used to satisfy needs that cannot be satisfied with consumer or capital goods, for example, police security in an area, lecturers, doctors, and lawyers.

4.1.3 The individual as consumer

All people have unique needs and businesses should attempt to satisfy these individual consumer needs. The decision to satisfy an individual's need is influenced by the resources (money) available to them. The more money a person has the more needs that person can satisfy.

4.1.4 The secretary/management assistant's understanding of human needs

To provide a high level of service to customers, you, as the secretary/management assistant, must understand each customer's unique needs.

To be able to achieve this, you should do the following:

- Identify exactly what the customer needs, for example, a meeting with the manager.
- Consider what options are available to meet this need, for example, a time when the manager is available.
- Provide the customer with the options that are available and let the customer decide between the various options.
- If the customer has not made a final decision, but is still considering two or three options, provide more information on each option to help the customer decide.

> **DEFINITION**
>
> **market** – a place where buyers and sellers meet to trade goods and/or services in exchange for money

- Once the customer has decided, confirm the decision by completing all the necessary paperwork.
- If the customer is not willing to accept the options, try to understand why the options do not meet the specific need.
- Provide all the necessary feedback to the manager and make the necessary changes to improve the organisation's goods or services.

4.1.5 Factors influencing consumer behaviour

Consumer behaviour is influenced by several different factor.

Individual factors (needs and attitudes)

Each person is unique and makes different buying decisions. For example, a person with blonde hair would normally only buy blonde hair dye, while a person with black hair will only buy black hair dye.

Perceptions

Buying decisions are often influenced by people's **perceptions**. For instance, if a person perceives that if a product has a high health risk, that person will not buy that product even though it may be very affordable. Similarly, a person's perception that an item is a quality product may make them buy the product, even though a cheaper alternative may be available.

Learning ability

A person's level of education can also influence the final buying decision. Some people take longer to make buying decisions as they consider all the factors before they buy. For example, an Office Practice graduate's decision on their first car will be influenced by what they can afford, what make of car they want, whether it will be better to buy a new car or a good second-hand car, the fuel efficiency of the car and the maintenance costs for such a car? Perhaps a Grade 8 student will not make buying decisions based on so many factors and may merely decide on what they can afford and is it cool to have.

Personality traits

The personality of the consumer can play a vital role in buying goods, especially those goods satisfying esteem or self-actualisation needs. An introverted or quiet person may

DEFINITION

perception – a way of regarding, understanding or interpreting something

not be too keen to buy a colourful floral print dress, but an extroverted person may love the look of it and the statement it makes.

The family

The family of the consumer can influence a consumer to make certain choices that are more acceptable to the family. For example, buying a safe new car for the family will require it to be big enough for all in the family to fit in the car and have all the necessary safety features. However, a single person may decide to buy either a two-door sports car or a motor cycle.

Reference groups

A person's buying decision can also be influenced by the person's culture, religion, or where the person lives (demographic). For example, the needs and wants of people in the United States differs vastly from someone from Swaziland. Similarly, an Italian's shoe choices differ greatly from an Eskimo's choice of shoes.

Income and standard of living

As mentioned previously, the higher a person's income, the more consumer and capital goods that individual will want. Income level also influences the standard of living. Workers use their wages or salaries to buy what they need or want and can afford. If that person receives a higher-paying job, then their buying pattern will also change.

Power break 4.1   INDIVIDUAL WORK

Match the examples below to the categories of goods that can satisfy human needs (consumer goods, capital goods or services).

Examples of goods	Categories of goods
1. Hairdresser	
2. Printer	
3. Burger and chips	
4. Services of a security company	
5. Coffee machine	
6. Housing	

UNIT 4.2 Marketing of products

This unit focuses on how the business goes about marketing its products and/or services to consumers and discusses the following:
- product positioning
- groups in the market
- classification of consumer products
- marketing strategy
- product life cycle.

4.2.1 Market segmentation

Market segmentation is where the business divides its consumer market into different sections or segments and then concentrates efforts on one or a few segments only. The process to determine the different market segments are as follows:
- Understand the different consumer needs from market research.
- Determine the marketing mix.
    - Confirm what the level of competition is in each segment including pricing of their products.
    - Determine which existing products or new products to sell in the segment.
    - Decide on how the business will advertise to the consumer (promotion).
    - Confirm where will be the best place to be closest to the customers and deciding on which method to use to get the product to the customer.
- Analyse which segments will be most profitable.
- Start selling to the chosen market segment.
- Review the performance in the market segment and make changes as needed.

4.2.2 Criteria for market segmentation

There are four common types of market segmentation, each with its own criteria.

The four common types of market segmentation
The following paragraphs describe the four most common types of market segmentation.

Geographical factors
The market is split based on where the customers are located. This can be the area in which the person lives or works, or the route along which the customer travels.

Demographical factors
The market is divided based on factors such as age, gender, income level, education, race, occupation and culture.

Psychographic factors
Here, the target market is segmented based on socio-economic class, personality, or lifestyle preference.

Behaviour factors
The market is divided up into type of behaviour shown by the consumers such as price sensitivity, loyalty and perception.

Other types of market segmentation
There are other ways of segmenting a target market:

Type of product
You will find an example of the type of product market segmentation in a retail store where the market segments can include men's wear, women's wear, children's wear, cellphones, make-up, and perfume.

Type of client/industry
Product market segmentation by the type of client/industry refers to segmentation by industry or undertaking, such as construction, insurance, banking, public transport, manufacturing, and mining.

4.2.3 Product positioning

Product positioning is when a business tries to influence a customer to choose its product or service brand instead of that of a competitor. When customers can choose from different brands of the same product, they will select a specific brand for specific reasons. For example, a clothing brand may use a famous sports star to advertise its brand. This will show the consumers that professionals use their products and it could do the same for the customer.

4.2.4 Different groups in the market

A market is a place where buyers and sellers meet to trade goods and/or services in exchange for money. We now explore the different groups that operate within the market.

Suppliers
Suppliers supply raw materials, goods and services to the business to offer to the market. Suppliers prefer to supply products or services to businesses that have a similar outlook regarding their products and services as this makes it an extension of their marketing to the end user. Suppliers also prefer businesses to pay on time and to have a positive corporate image.

Consumers
Consumers are people who are willing to pay money for goods and services offered by a business. Consumers will look at different products and services until they find the product or service that can satisfy their need.

Competitors

Competitors are businesses that offer similar products and services and provide a consumer with a choice for that product or service to satisfy a need.

Market leaders

Market leaders are companies that are the preferred suppliers of a product or service. For example, Coca-Cola are the world market leaders for bottled cooldrinks. Their marketing strategy is more aggressive to maintain market leadership and they advertise aggressively, especially during the summer months.

Challengers

Challengers are businesses that compete the closest with the market leader and want to take the market-leader position. They have an aggressive marketing strategy to persuade consumers to buy their brand. For example, Apple are challenging Samsung to become the leading brand in the global smartphone market and will usually arrange a large media launch to highlight the benefits of their new products.

Followers

Followers are the businesses that compete with the market leaders and the challengers but are not yet ready to challenge for the market-leader position. For example, Huawei and Hi Sense are cellphone manufacturers but are not close to competing with Samsung or Apple.

Avoiders

Avoiders are businesses that are in the market but that do not actively go out to gain business from clients. They avoid the competition as in most cases the market is not their main source of income.

Middlemen

In certain markets, there is someone or some company that either acts on behalf of the seller or on behalf of the buyer. These middlemen will negotiate on behalf of their principal to gain the sale or purchase. The middlemen earn a commission for their service. For example, if a cruise ship wants to buy supplies in a foreign country the ship's buyer will contact a ship's agent with the list of their requirements. The ship's agent will then buy all the supplies and have it ready when the ship arrives in the foreign harbour.

4.2.5 Classification of consumer products

Consumer goods are products used by consumers or households to satisfy their needs. Consumer goods fall into different categories.

Durable goods

Durable goods can be used repeatedly. These goods include items such as furniture, cars, equipment, plates and cutlery. Marketing and selling durable goods requires personal selling with a strong service component. High profits with guarantees and warranties are normally included in the price of the product.

Non-durable goods

Non-durable goods are products that have a short life-span. They can be used once or a few times before they must be replaced. Examples include food, toiletries, stationery and petrol. These goods are purchased regularly, and consumers have a strong brand preference. The goods tend to be available at many outlets, usually have low profit margins and require little sales effort to sell to consumers.

Convenience goods

Convenience goods are familiar goods like groceries and newspapers. The products are sold at different outlets.

Convenience goods are:

- staple goods, which include products like bread, milk, mealie meal, rice, fruits and vegetables
- impulse purchases or products that are bought without thought, and include sweets, chocolates, chips and nuts
- emergency goods, which include products like medicine and plasters that are bought in the event of an emergency or to treat a medical condition.

When marketing convenience goods, a marketer must consider the following:

- Producers tend to be responsible for advertising and promotion of the products.
- Products are bought on a self-service basis. This makes effective packaging essential.
- Retailers carry different brands of convenience products and are not keen to advertise individual products.
- Quality and prices of competing brands tend to be similar.

Shopping goods

Shopping goods include products like clothing and jewellery. These goods tend to have a higher unit value than convenience products and are bought less frequently.

Speciality products

Speciality products include products like cars, computers and cameras. Such products have unique characteristics and are often expensive.

Figure 4.3 An expensive camera is a speciality product.

4.2.6 Marketing strategies

Marketing strategies are focussed on different means of satisfying customer needs. This section discusses the strategies of branding, packaging, pricing, distribution, advertising and promotions. We also look at the important aspect of product life cycle.

Branding

Branding, also known as trademarking, is an element of product policy and is closely linked to and connected with promotion and packaging. A brand is a name, term, design, symbol or any other feature that distinguishes one marketer's product or service from others. Branding involves giving a product an identity.

Packaging

Packaging refers to a group of activities that involves design manufacturing and filling a container or wrapper with the product so that it can be protected, stored, handled, transported, identified and marketed.

Pricing

Price is an element of the marketing mix and is a single common source of conflict between suppliers and potential consumers. Price is determined by a compromise between the forces of demand and supply and is the amount a consumer pays for a product or service to satisfy a need.

Distribution

Distribution is about the producer finding:

- the best outlets to make products available to consumers
- the most economical way to get products to the end customer.

Here are different distribution channels that can be used:

Producer to consumer

The producer sells directly to the consumer. For example, Steer's sells a hamburger to a customer.

Producer to retailer to consumer

The producer first sells to a retailer who then sells to the consumer. An example is Nike selling to Total Sports who sells to a consumer.

Producer to wholesaler to retailer to consumer

The producer sells to a wholesaler; the wholesaler sells to a retailer; and the retailer sells to the consumer. For example, Tiger Brands sells cold meats to Makro. Makro sells the cold meats to Woolworths. Woolworths sells to the consumer.

Producer to wholesaler to consumer

The producer sells to the wholesaler, who then sells to the consumer. For example, Unilever sells soap to Jumbo Cash & Carry and Jumbo Cash & Carry sells to the consumer.

The choice of distribution channel depends on the whether a product is durable or non-durable. Durable products and have a long distribution channel. Non-durable products have shorter distribution channels as they have a short life span. The producer will also have to decide which means of transport to use along the distribution channel. For example, a producer who sells to a consumer based in another city or country can either send the product using road transport, rail transport, air transport or sea transport. Each transport means will attract a different cost and will impact on how profitable the product is.

Advertising

Advertising is the group of activities concerned with creating awareness, generating interest and a creating a desire for a product or service. It is controlled and paid, non-personal, outward marketing communication about a product or service by a company or individual aimed at a particular market. A company can advertise in many ways and can use various channels, including:

- television
- radio
- newspapers
- magazines
- websites
- flyers
- brochures
- emails
- social media.

Promotions

Sales promotions are marketing communication methods not classified as advertising, but also aimed at changing consumer behaviour.

Promotion has three objectives:

- To inform potential consumers who have no knowledge of products or services offered by a business.
- To persuade potential consumers to buy products or services on offer.
- To remind existing and potential consumers that products and services are still available.

4.2.7 Product life cycle

The **product life cycle** has four defined stages. Each stage has its own characteristics that mean different things for businesses. This cycle has a distinctive beginning, middle and end.

All products start out with an idea or concept. The concept or idea then enters a research and development (R&D) phase. After the R&D phase, the product enters the life cycle, starting with an introductory stage, as shown in Figure 4.4, which shows sales over the life of va product.

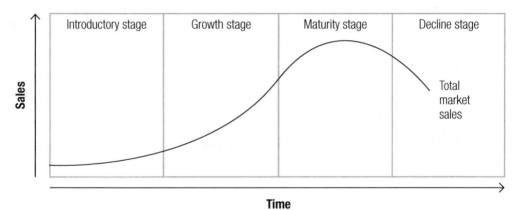

Figure 4.4 Products go from idea to decline over time.

> **DEFINITION**
>
> **product life cycle** – four very clearly defined stages, each with its own characteristics

Table 4.2 describes the stages in the life cycle of a product.

Table 4.2 The stages in the life cycle of a product

Stage of life cycle	Description of stage
Introductory stage	Once the product has been created it will be introduced into the market.
Growth stage	As more and more consumers see the benefits of the product, sales increase.
Maturity stage	The maturity phase is where sales reach their highest levels.
Declining stage	Once the sales start to decline the product enters the declining phase until the product is either upgraded or is withdrawn from the market.

Power break 4.2   INDIVIDUAL WORK

You are the secretary of Cell Moby and the company is in the process of introducing their latest product onto the market. You have been instructed to support the marketing manager with the launch event and you have been put in charge of the invitations for the event.

Create an invitation that covers the following information:
1   Company or customer name (who you want to invite)
2   Purpose of the event
3   Date, time and place of the event
4   RSVP date
5   Dress code.

UNIT 4.3 **Types of business ownership**

A secretary/management assistant needs to understand of the different types of business ownership, namely:
- sole proprietor
- partnership
- private company
- public company
- close corporation
- informal businesses.

This unit covers the founding procedures and characteristics of each of these types of business ownership.

4.3.1 Sole proprietor

A sole proprietor or sole trader is a form of enterprise owned and managed by an individual. Businesses such as coffee shops, photographers, plumbers and electricians could well operate as sole traders.

Figure 4.5 Many coffee shops operate as sole traders.

Founding procedures

The sole trader business is the easiest business to get started. The founding procedures are as follows:

- The owner provides the capital to start the business.
- The owner decides on the unique trading name of the business. This name may not be the same as an existing business.
- The owner must obtain a trading licence from the local municipality before beginning to trade.

Characteristics

The characteristics of a sole trader are as follows:

- The business is run in the name of the owner or under a trading name given by the owner.
- The owner is responsible for the debts of the business.
- There are no shareholders in the company.
- The owner is the manager of the business and all staff will report to him or her.
- All profits and losses go to the owner of the business.
- The business does not pay tax, but the owners of these sole trader businesses must include all income and expenses of the business in their personal tax submissions.
- The business only exists while the owner is alive. If the owner dies, the business ends.

4.3.2 Partnership

A partnership is a business where two or more people conduct a business together. Many accounting practices, law firms and doctors operate as partnerships.

Founding procedures

The founding procedures for a partnership are as follows:

- Two to a maximum of twenty partners provide the capital, labour and skills to start the business.
- The partners provide the name of the business, which may not be the same as an existing business.
- The partners enter into a partnership agreement that covers all aspects of the business, including capital contribution, banking arrangements, profit and losses, salaries, bonuses, leave and withdrawals from the business.

Figure 4.6 Partners enter into an agreement that covers all aspects of the business.

Characteristics

The characteristics of a partnership are as follows:

- The business is easy to set up as only a partnership agreement is needed to set it up.
- Partnerships are preferred by professionals wanting to share skills and knowledge.
- The partners are jointly and severally liable for all the debts of the business. If the business fails to pay a debt, the **creditor** can recover the outstanding amount from any of the partners.

> **DEFINITION**
>
> **creditor –** someone that the business owes money to

- There are no shareholders in a partnership, however, the partnership is governed by the partnership agreement.
- Each partner provides the skills, labour and management in the partnership.
- Partners share profits and losses in accordance with the terms of the partnership agreement.
- All partners must include their share of the income and expenses of the business in their respective tax returns.
- The partnership agreement ends if any of the partners dies or withdraws from the partnership.

4.3.3 Private company

A private company is a business held under private ownership. Examples of private companies include national and multinational companies like Clover SA (Pty) Ltd, Shell SA (Pty) Ltd and Oxford University Press Southern Africa (Pty) Ltd.

Founding procedures

The founding procedures of a private company are as follows:
- A private company is formed when at least one **person** but not more than fifty establish a business registered with the Companies and Intellectual Property Commission (CIPC).
- A Memorandum of Incorporation is completed, and the prescribed fee is paid to the CIPC.
- The shareholders contribute capital to form the company and are issued with a shareholder's certificate to confirm ownership of a share in the business.
- All shareholders are recorded in a shareholder's register.
- The name of the business is registered and must end with the words '(Pty) Ltd' (Proprietary Limited). The name may not be the same as any existing business.
- The private company has a separate legal identity and is responsible for all the debts and losses it may experience.
- The owners (shareholders) have limited liability and cannot be sued in their own capacity for the debts or losses of the company.
- The private company must appoint an independent auditor to audit its annual financial statements.
- The private company is required to hold an annual general meeting with all shareholders to discuss the performance and financial statements.
- Shares in the private company can only be bought and sold with the permission of the board of directors.

> **DEFINITION**
>
> **person** – includes people and other legal persona (companies or close corporations)

Figure 4.7 A private company must appoint an independent auditor to audit the business' annual financial statements.

Characteristics

The characteristics of a private company are as follows:

- A private company is managed by a board of directors who can appoint or change a management team to run the company.
- All profits and losses belong to the company and are retained in the company.
- All financial statements in a private company must be lodged with the CIPC.
- All changes to directors of a private company must be registered with the CIPC.
- All changes to the registered business address of a private company must be lodged with the CIPC.
- Shareholders in a private company have a right to vote in board meetings based on the number of shares that they hold in the company.
- Shareholders are paid a dividend from the profits generated from the company's business. The board of directors will declare a dividend once the financial statements have been signed off (audited and lodged with the CIPC).
- Shareholders cannot withdraw funds from the capital they contributed unless they sell some of their shares in the company to someone else.
- A private company is responsible to pay corporate tax on the income less the expenses of the business. Shareholders only pay personal tax on the dividends that have been paid to them during the tax year. Shareholders may have to pay capital gains tax when they sell their shares in the company.
- A private company continues to operate even if a shareholder dies or sells their shares in the company.

Did you know? The following obligations are required by the CIPC for private companies:

- company records
- accounting records
- appointment and rotation of auditors
- annual returns
- financial statements and independent reviews
- appointment of a social and ethics committee
- solvency and reckless trading
- obligation to notify the CIPC of certain changes.

4.3.4 Public company

A public company is a company whose shares can be bought by the public. Examples of public companies include Discovery Ltd, African Rainbow Minerals Ltd and Golden Arrow Ltd.

Founding procedures

The founding procedures for a public company are as follows:

- A minimum of seven persons are required to start a public company
- The name of the company must end with the word 'Ltd'. This is the abbreviation for 'Limited'.
- In South Africa, shares in a public company are traded (bought and sold) on the Johannesburg Stock Exchange.
- A public company has a separate legal identity and the company is responsible for all its debts and losses.
- The owners (shareholders) have limited liability and cannot be sued in their own capacity for the debts or losses of the company.
- A public company must appoint an independent auditor to audit the annual financial statements.
- A public company is required to hold an annual general meeting with all shareholders to discuss the performance and financial statements of the company.

Figure 4.8 In South Africa, shares in a public company are bought and sold on the Johannesburg Stock Exchange.

Characteristics

The characteristics of a public company are as follows:

- A public company is governed by a board of directors who can appoint a management team to run the company on a day-to-day basis.
- A public company is a separate legal entity and all profits and losses belong to the company.
- Shareholders in a public company can vote in a board meeting based on the number of shares that they hold in the company.
- All changes to directors in a public company must be registered with the CIPC.
- All changes to the registered business address of the public company must be lodged with the CIPC.
- Shareholders cannot withdraw funds from the capital they contributed unless they sell some of their shares in the company to someone else.
- A public company must submit their audited financial statements with the CIPC.
- A public company can declare dividends from the profits generated during the financial year. This is paid to shareholders based on the number of shares that they own in the company.
- A public company must be registered as a taxpayer and pays corporate tax on the income less the expenses of the company during the tax year. The shareholders pay personal tax on the dividends that were paid to them. The shareholders may have to pay capital gains tax if they sell their shares in the company.
- A public company continues to exist even if shareholders sell their shares in the company or die.

> **Did you know?** There are other types of companies governed by the CIPC, such as state-owned companies, non-profit companies and external (foreign) companies.

4.3.5 Close corporation

A close corporation (CC) is a company with shares held by a few individuals who are usually closely associated with the business. Examples of CCs include some small and medium businesses such as engineering firms, law firms and printing firms.

Founding procedures

The founding procedures for a CC are as follows:

- A CC is founded by lodging of a founding statement (CK2) and a certificate of incorporation (CK1) with the required fee to the CIPC.
- Between one to ten members each provide a capital contribution.
- The name of the company must end with CC and must not be the same as an existing business name.
- The CC must appoint an accounting officer to take care of the financial reporting on the company.

Characteristics

The characteristics of a CC are as follows:

- The members of the CC own and manage the company.
- A company cannot be a member of a CC.
- Members can withdraw their capital contribution at any time.
- A CC is a separate legal entity and all profits and losses belong to the company.
- The CC must be registered as a taxpayer and pays corporate tax on the income less the expenses of the company during the tax year. The members pay personal tax on the dividends that were paid to them. The members may have to pay capital gains tax when they sell their shares in the CC.
- A CC continues to exist even after a member sells their shares or dies.
- Members must first offer their shares to existing members before they can sell them to anyone else.

4.3.6 Informal business

The main reason why people decide to start an informal business is due to unemployment and having no alternative source of income. People would find something to sell. They sell one item and keep some of the profits to buy new stock to sell.

According to a 2013 Statistics South Africa (Stats SA) survey, turnover levels and profit margins are relatively small for most informal businesses. In 2013, 52,3% had a turnover of R1 500 or below in the month prior to the survey and only 14,6% had sales above R6 000. Net profits for 64,9% of businesses were also low – R1 500 or lower in the month prior to the survey – and only 9,2% of businesses made net profits above R6 000 (Stats SA, 2013).

Types of informal businesses

Some examples of informal businesses are hawkers, stokvels, spaza shops and flea markets.

Hawker

We see hawkers selling their goods from pavement stalls of sorts or beside a road. They usually advertising their goods by shouting. They either grow their own stock or buy from a wholesaler to sell to their customers. They sell small items like mealies, doilies, brooms and dusters.

Stokvel

A stokvel is started when all stokvel members contribute a fixed amount on a regular basis, normally monthly. Each member gets a turn to receive all the contributions for that period. For example, if there are five stokvel members, each contributing R2 000 per month, each member will have a month where they receive R10 000 (5 × R2 000). A stokvel relies on members keeping to their promise to contribute each month until all members have had a turn to receive the pool of contributions. The stokvel ends when all members have received their month's share. New members can only join when the new cycle of contributions begins.

Spaza shop

A spaza shop is like a hawker except it is usually located in someone's home or an empty container that has stock of all staples and impulse items. The business is like a sole trader as the owner runs the business on a full-time basis to make ends meet.

Flea market

Flea markets are places where informal traders display their different stock items in a hired stall normally covered by a gazebo. The stock is packed on a table and the owner/salesperson usually has a chair to sit on when there is no business. Customers negotiate a price for items that are on sale. The goods sold at a flea market include handbags, books, shoes, T-shirts, sports shoes (takkies), stationery, toys and plants.

Figure 4.9 Flea markets allow you to sell almost anything.

Founding procedure

It is very easy to start an informal business.

- The owners do not register the business.
- They do not have a registered business address.
- They normally do not declare their income from their business.

Characteristics

The characteristics of an informal business are as follows:

- Most informal businesses (except for some spaza shops) do not have a name for their business.
- They do not keep records of their income and expenses. The money generated from sales is used to buy new stock and to pay for transport and staff costs.

- The business is small and can be moved to a new location without much hassle.
- Informal business owners do not usually have access to funds to run the business and the owner pays for the day-to-day operations.
- As they supply staples in the community, they need the local community to keep the business going.

4.3.7 Why does a secretary/management assistant need to know about the types of business ownerships?

The secretary/management assistant deals with customers from different business ownerships and each has unique needs and challenges. The way a sole trader is handled will differ to the way a public company is dealt with. If the secretary must talk to the key decision makers in a business, the type of business will influence the way the secretary/management assistant approaches the task at hand.

The secretary's/management assistant's job description and job routine will also be differ depending on the type of business. This may include differences in:
- office procedures
- decision making processes that need to be followed
- career growth opportunities
- interactions with clients
- salary and benefits
- leave and working hours.

Power break 4.3 INDIVIDUAL WORK

Do some research on an established sole proprietor and a partnership in your community. Collect the following information about them.

1 What is the name of the proprietorship and partnership?
2 What product or service do they sell?
3 Who are their competition?
4 What makes the sole proprietorship different from a partnership?

UNIT 4.4 Public utility undertakings

A public utility company/undertaking is a business that provides consumers with basic services such as water, electricity, refuse collection, telecommunications, infrastructure, or transportation. As these services are considered strategic most governments prefer to control the running of these businesses. These utility undertakings are normally run by a local municipality or by a state-owned enterprise (SOE).

Examples of these utility undertakings in South Africa are Eskom, Rand Water Board, Golden Arrow Bus Service, SANRAL and Telkom.

Figure 4.10 The Koeberg nuclear power station is a state-owned utility company.

4.4.1 Need for utility undertakings

Utility undertakings provide services that are key to satisfying primary human needs, and in some instances, even secondary human needs.

To provide the service, the local municipality or SOE needs a large capital investment, normally provided from taxes collected. Once the infrastructure for the utility has been established, the utility either sells the service to the local municipality or directly to the consumer.

4.4.2 Role of utility undertakings

As mentioned, a public utility provides consumers with basic services. Basic services are sold to consumers irrespective of their level of income and in some instances are provided at lower rates to pensioners or **indigent** households.

As most SOEs have a **monopoly** in the supply of basic services, they can control the price levels that these services are sold at.

In many instances, the capital outlay to provide basic services does not match the income that is generated from selling the services and could lead to the SOEs running at losses for many years. Governments usually absorb these losses as it is a basic service to the bulk of the population.

Power break 4.4   GROUP WORK

In groups of three, identify six different types of utilities the college uses on a day-to-day basis and list the main service providers for the utilities you identified.

DEFINITIONS

indigent – needy or very poor person

monopoly – when the main supplier has the greater market share and can manipulate the market when they want to

WHAT DO WE KNOW AND WHERE TO NEXT?

This module covered human needs. We looked at the origin of needs, the different types of needs, satisfying these needs and the individual as a consumer. We also discussed why it is necessary for the secretary/management assistant to know about human needs.

The module then examined consumer behaviour, specifically the effect of individual needs and attitudes, perception, learning ability, personality traits, the family, reference group, income and standard of living.

Unit 4.2 covered the marketing of products and investigated market segmentation and its criteria, product positioning, different groups in the market and the classification of consumer products. We also considered different types of marketing strategy and the concept of product life cycle.

The module then discussed types of business ownership (sole proprietor, partnership, public company, private company, close corporation, and informal businesses) and mentioned the founding procedures and characteristics for each of the types. The module concluded with a discussion on the need and role of public utility undertakings.

The next module focuses on human resources in the workplace and includes the aspects of recruitment, appointment, induction and training and development.

Revisiting the learning objectives

Now that you have completed this module you should have achieved the learning objectives listed in the table below.

Learning objective	What you have learned	✔
Explain human needs with reference to the following: • origin of needs • different types of needs (external and internal) • goals (things to satisfy needs) • the individual as a consumer.	Human needs stem from primary needs for food, clothing, air, etc. to self-actualisation needs, such as, morality, creativity or acceptance of facts. The goods that satisfy needs are categorised as consumer goods, capital goods and services.	☐
Briefly state how knowledge of human needs would affect a secretary's/management assistant's view of customers.	As customers are unique, secretaries/management assistants follow the due process to determine a customer's needs and provide all the information to help them satisfy those needs.	☐

continued on next page …

Learning objective	What you have learned	✔
Explain in detail the determinants of consumer behaviour: • individual factors (needs and attitudes) • perception • learning ability • personality traits • the family • reference groups • income and standard of living.	Consumer behaviour differs due to individual qualities, such as tastes, feelings and learning ability. A consumer's choice of product can be affected by the personality of the consumer, family ties, income and standard of living. The various role players within the market will also affect the choice of product or service.	☐
Briefly explain market segmentation, product positioning, different groups in the market and classification of consumer products.	Market segmentation helps a business to streamline its offer to specific customers. Product positioning assists the customer to choose one brand over another. Whether the company is a market leader, challenger, follower or avoider will influence its marketing strategy.	☐
Explain in detail the following aspects of a marketing strategy: • branding • packaging • pricing • distribution • advertising • promotions • product life cycle.	A marketing strategy focuses on different means to satisfy customer needs. • Branding is about giving a name, term, design or symbol to a product that makes it unique. • Packaging involves design, manufacturing and filling a container or wrapper with a product so it can be protected, stored, transported, identified and marketed. • Pricing is the compromise between supply and demand. • Distribution is about using the best outlet for products and/or the most economical way to get the product to the consumer. • Advertising is used to create awareness, generate interest and create a desire for a product or service. • Promotions are aimed at changing consumer behaviour. • A product life cycle spans over time, from idea, to a decline in sales.	☐
Briefly explain the founding procedure for the following business enterprises: • sole proprietor • partnership • public company • private company • close corporation • informal.	Business enterprises have different founding procedures: • Sole traders need a trading licence from the municipality. • Partnerships need a partnership agreement. • Private companies require a memorandum of incorporation. • Public companies must be listed on the stock exchange. • Close corporations require a founding statement and a certificate of incorporation. • Informal businesses usually do not need a trading licence but may need one to trade at a flea market.	☐

continued on next page ...

Learning objective	What you have learned	✔
Explain the characteristics of the following business enterprises: • sole proprietor • partnership • public company • private company • close corporation • informal.	Business enterprises have different requirements regarding their name, capital contribution, withdrawal of funds, tax paid, responsibility for the debts and losses of the business enterprise, and continuity when a share/membership is sold, or a person dies.	☐
Briefly explain why a secretary/management assistant has to have a basic knowledge of the types of business ownership.	The secretary/management assistant will benefit from knowing the different types of business ownership as it influences the job description, salary, benefits, working hours and the interactions with customers.	☐
Briefly explain the need for and the role of utility undertakings (giving examples).	Public utility undertakings provide basic services, such as water, electricity, refuse removal, infrastructure and telecommunications. They help in meeting human needs. For example, water and electricity form part of primary human needs and impact on secondary human needs.	☐

Assessment

1. Multiple choice

Choose the correct answer from the various options provided. Choose only A, B, C, or D and write it next to the question number.

1.1 Retrenchment is when the economy of the country or the growth of the company _____ .

    A   decreases

    B   depreciates

    C   steadily moves

    D   increases

1.2 The most similar type of ownership to the private company is a _____ .

    A   sole trader

    B   partnership

    C   close corporation

    D   public company

1.3 Which one of the following is not a human need?

    A   a natural need

    B   an essential need

    C   a services/goods need

    D   a luxury need

1.4 Income and education are examples of _____ .

    A   demographical factors

    B   geographical factors

    C   psychographic factors

    D   market segmentation

1.5 _____ consists of needs at the highest level where people discover themselves and their full potential.

    A   Self-actualisation

    B   Safety

    C   Esteem

    D   Physiological

(5 × 1 = 5)

[5]

2. True or false

Choose whether the following statements are true or false. Write down the number of the question and 'true' or 'false'.

2.1 Marketing production is the process whereby the total market is identified and divided into subgroups or segments with similar needs.

2.2 Suppliers is the competition between two companies to satisfy consumer needs.

2.3 Social media is the most commonly used method of advertising.

2.4 One of the characteristics of a public/open company is that a board of directors manages the company.

2.5 Marketing production is the process whereby the total market is identified and divided into subgroups or segments with similar needs.

$(5 \times 1 = 5)$

[5]

3. Match the columns

Choose a description from Column B that matches the word/item in Column A. Write only the letter (A–E) next to the question number.

Column A	Column B
3.1 Consumer behaviour	A. A process whereby the total market is identified and divided into subgroups or segments of similar needs
3.2 Satisfaction of needs	B. The desire or craving for something (goods or services) that gives us physical, social or psychological satisfaction
3.3 Market segmentation	C. The behavioural pattern of decision making individuals or groups of individuals directly involved in the identification, purchasing and usage of goods and services to satisfy their needs
3.4 Need	D. An example of this is jewellery
3.5 Speciality goods	E. Influencing the decision-making process of the consumer

$(5 \times 1 = 5)$

[5]

4. Short questions

4.1 Identify the type of ownership from the following statements:

    4.1.1 Limited capital is needed to start a business.

    4.1.2 The business is normally service oriented.

    4.1.3 One to ten people can form this type of ownership.

    4.1.4 A board of directors manages the business.

    4.1.5 The maximum number of members is by law restricted to 20. $(5 \times 2 = 10)$

4.2 Explain the following terms used in business:

    4.2.1 marketing

    4.2.2 trademark

    4.2.3 distribution

    4.2.4 purchasing

    4.2.5 consumer $(5 \times 2 = 10)$

4.3 Identify the type of ownership based on the following statements:

    4.3.1 Limited capital is needed to start a business.

    4.3.2 The business is normally service oriented.

    4.3.3 One to ten people can form this type of ownership.

    4.3.4 A board of directors manages the business.

    4.3.5 The maximum number of members is restricted by law to 20. $(5 \times 2 = 10)$

[30]

5. Long questions

5.1 Explain how the factors of production can influence the distribution of goods/services in a business. (5)

5.2 Distinguish between companies with shared capital and companies with no shared capital and give one example of each. (5)

5.3 Discuss in detail the founding procedures and characteristics of private companies. (5 × 2 = 10)

5.4 Discuss the demographical factors that influence market segmentation. (5 × 2 = 10)

[30]

6. Case study

Study the picture below and answer the questions that follow.

6.1 Name the type of ownership in the picture above. (2)

6.2 Give one example of the type of ownership named in Question 6.1 (2)

6.3 Give two founding procedures for the type of ownership named in Question 6.1. (4)

6.4 Give two ways in which the informal sector entrepreneurs advertise their business. (4)

6.5 Discuss the characteristics of the informal sector as a type of ownership. (5)

6.6 In your opinion, does this type of ownership require a management assistant? Motivate your answer. (4)

6.7 Give two examples of informal business sectors in your area. (4)

[25]

Grand total: 100 marks

HUMAN RESOURCES PROVISIONING

This module considers the following aspects of human resources provisioning:

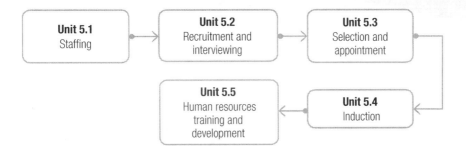

Unit 5.1
Staffing

Unit 5.2
Recruitment and interviewing

Unit 5.3
Selection and appointment

Unit 5.5
Human resources training and development

Unit 5.4
Induction

Learning objectives

After completing this module, you should be able to do the following:

- Explain human resources planning.
- Explain recruitment as an important function of human resources provisioning.
- Explain paper selection of applicants (in order to compile a shortlist).
- Explain the procedures and documentation used in the final stage before the appointment of new staff.
- Explain interviewing of applicants for a vacant post.
- After having viewed a video on an interview for a post, identify the advantages of a successful interview, the pitfalls, and problems of a poorly conducted interview as well as the do's and don'ts concerning interviews.
- Briefly elucidate on the selection policy and procedure pertaining to human resource management.
- Briefly explain equal employment opportunities and affirmative action as components of a selection policy for human resource management.
- Elucidate on the necessity of the correct placement of the correct person in a particular post.
- Explain the appointment of a successful applicant.
- Explain the importance of an induction programme for newly appointed staff for both the organisation and the employee.

continued on next page ...

Learning objectives

- Briefly explain why it is necessary to do a follow-up after the induction programme.
- Explain training of secretarial staff (secretaries/management assistants and support staff).
- Briefly explain the difference between training and development.
- Explain development programmes/techniques for secretaries/management assistants.

Key terms

affirmative action
human resources
human resources
  department
incumbent

interview
job analysis
mentor
objective
probationary

psychometric test
recruitment
staffing
tacit
written offer

Starting point

Roland wants to prepare Verushna for her future in a possible supervisory role or even an executive secretary and he is highlighting to her that the secretarial field as a career has many sides that need to be understood in order for the junior secretary/management assistant to achieve the goal of holding a top position within this field. One side that Verushna needs to understand is how an organisation follows processes and procedures to ensure that the right candidate is placed in the right position. This helps the person to achieve an elevated level of job satisfaction and helps the organisation to achieve its own goals and objectives. So how do you move from the successful graduate as pictured in Figure 5.1 below to be the executive assistant to a CEO?

Figure 5.1 My career starts after graduation.

UNIT 5.1 Staffing

This first unit discusses the topics of **staffing**, which includes **human resources** (HR) planning and human resources forecasting. The unit includes a case study on staffing in the secretarial division of a business undertaking.

5.1.1 Human resources planning

The main goal of human resources planning is to match the number and quality of employees with the continually changing needs of the organisation. Human resources planning does three important things:

- It analyses the current human resources in an organisation.
- It makes forecasts about what personnel are needed.
- It draws up plans to ensure that these needs are met.

This planning is vital as it shows personnel shortages so new employees can be recruited and selected to fill the gaps. HR planning also finds excess staff and this helps keep the labour costs down.

Understanding the skills levels of current staff helps the **human resources department** set up training programmes to help staff develop their talents and enable them to contribute further to the organisation's goals. HR planning also ensures that the organisation keeps up with social, economic, legislative, and technological trends that impact on how it performs. **Recruitment** and training are expensive, so it is important that HR has a clear picture of what it is to do so that the organisation can include these costs in its operating budget.

Good HR planning will ensure that the department functions are not interrupted by skills shortages or a lack of workers. It improves employee morale because the organisation will work more efficiently and profitably. Employees will be loyal to an organisation that gives them opportunities to grow in their jobs.

DEFINITIONS

staffing – the selection and training of individuals for specific job functions and making them responsible to perform those job functions

human resources – the people who make up the workforce of an organisation, business sector, or economy

human resources department – the company department responsible for finding, screening, recruiting, and training job applicants, as well as administering employee-benefit programmes

recruitment – the process of finding and hiring the best-qualified candidate to fill a position in the organisation

---

5.1.2 Steps in the HR planning process

Table 5.1 shows the steps in the HR planning process.

Table 5.1 The steps in the HR planning process

Serial	Step in the process	Description
1	Clarify strategic objectives.	Analyse organisational objectives in various fields, such as production, marketing, finance, and sales, to get an idea about the work to be done in the future.
2	Analyse the environment.	Do an inventory of the number, ability, performance, and potential of current human resources.
3	Find the gaps.	Forecast the organisation's current and future human resource needs and show possible skills shortages. Check whether the positions can be filled internally or if they should be advertised externally.
4	Develop a plan.	Determine the most important human resources needs and decide what strategies will be used to meet them. The HR plan is aimed at recruitment, training, or interdepartmental transfers.
5	Implement plan and monitor progress.	Measure, check and report on how the plan is being implemented and the effect it is having on the operation of the organisation. Show further changes in the environment that need changes in the plan.

5.1.3 Human resource forecasting

Human resource forecasting is the way in which the organisation tries to predict:
* the number, type, and quality of staff that they would need in the future
* the range of tasks that the positions will handle
* the skills, knowledge, aptitude, and experience needed by the successful candidate.

Job analysis

Job analysis is an **objective** and comprehensive study of a specific position to:
* identify the tasks that make up the job
* determine the conditions under which the tasks are performed
* establish the job requirements in terms of, aptitude, skills, knowledge, attitude, and physical condition of the employee.

Job analysis allows HR to create job descriptions and job specifications, which are important in recruitment and employee selection.

> **DEFINITIONS**
>
> **job analysis** – the process of gathering and analysing information about the content and the human requirements of jobs, as well as, the context in which jobs are performed
>
> **objective (verb)** – not influenced by personal feelings or opinions in considering and representing facts

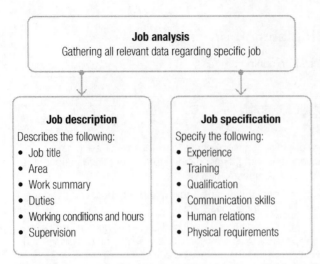

Figure 5.2 Job analysis helps develop a job description and a job specification.

Job analysis is used for:
- workforce planning, which decides what jobs are performed and required
- remuneration planning, which decides where and at what level in the organisation each job is positioned
- recruitment, selection and placement, which aims to match the right person to with the right job
- performance appraisal, which is the evaluation and appraisal of whether an individual is effectively pursuing the organisation's aim and objectives
- employee health and safety, which shows the working environment of each job
- identifying and setting up lines of responsibility and authority
- training and development, which helps find employees needing added training and development to meet the expected performance standards of their jobs
- individual job satisfaction, which helps HR discover whether employees are unhappy about their jobs and what aspects they would like to change
- organisational re-engineering, which examines the business processes and tries to arrange them to make the organisation more efficient.

Job description
A job description describes a specific job, gives an overview of the purpose of the job, and defines the nature of the job. A job description focuses on the essential functions of the job. It details what is done, how it is done, and why it is done.

Job descriptions answer the following questions:
- How often these functions and tasks are performed?
- How much time is spent on these functions?
- What happens if the job is not done?

Job descriptions are important because they:
- make it clear to employees what employers expect from them
- give a basis for measuring job performance

- list the activities, duties and responsibilities covered by different jobs and allow organisations to recruit, train and develop employees effectively
- are not open to interpretation and can function as a reference in case of employee/employer disputes
- are objective descriptions of what is expected and can be used for appraisals and performance reviews.

Job specification

A job specification focuses on the person doing the job and shows the personal traits, the experience, training, qualifications, communication skills, human relations and physical requirements needed for a specific job.

A job specification should include the following:

- Education – the required level of education that employees must have achieved.
- Training – the kind of training should have been completed.
- Skills – the abilities needed for the job.

Figure 5.3 A job specification includes the level of education that employees must have achieved.

- Experience – the he specific experience needed for the job.
- Initiative – the level of initiative that is expected of the employee.
- Emotional characteristics – the emotional characteristics that the employee will need in the job.
- Communication skills – the communication skills needed for the job.
- Physical qualities – the specific physical skills or abilities needed in the job.

Job enhancement

Job enhancement relates to added power, independence, and control over job performance. It means that the job includes responsibilities that have not been included in the job description.

Job enhancement takes place under the following circumstances:

- When some work is repetitive and expanding, job enhancement will motivate the staff involved.
- Job enhancement occurs during business restructuring exercises when positions are made redundant and the responsibilities are given to other employees.

- Job enhancement could result from the introduction of modern technology and processes that change the activities and work patterns in a job.
- Job enhancement occurs following a job evaluation where it is discovered that the position needs added responsibilities or needs to be downgraded.
- Job enhancement occurs when management decides to give a worker added responsibility.
- Job enhancement occurs when coaching an employee in preparation for a new job as part of the employee's career path plan.

Job enrichment

Job enrichment happens when there are added responsibilities assigned to the position resulting in increased job satisfaction. This could occur when:
- the employee is given increased responsibilities
- there is job shadowing by a senior employee
- the job allows for personal growth and development
- the job has an increased workload
- tasks are automated
- the employee has control over the given resources.

Power break 5.1   INDIVIDUAL WORK

Sam Sithelo, the managing director of High-Cents Television is faced with a problem of adding a new junior secretary for the Atlantis branch of the company. The high-definition television has seen rapid growth over the last five years and demand for the High-Cents Television is at an all-time high. The company has been growing rapidly and is opening two new regional branches. Sam is just not getting to do the necessary paperwork for this position. No recruitment of internal staff is possible. He has asked you, as his executive secretary, to please help as his programme is just too busy.

1 Compile a human resource forecast for the position. It should include the following:
  a) a comprehensive job analysis of the position
  b) a complete job description and job specification for the position.
2 Discuss how job enhancement and job enrichment can help to raise the level of the position in the organisation and give greater job satisfaction.

UNIT 5.2 Recruitment and interviewing

Following human resource planning and the human resource forecasting, the next phase in the process is the recruitment and **interviewing** phase.

5.2.1 Recruitment

As mentioned previously, recruitment is the process of finding and hiring the best-qualified candidate to fill a position in the organisation. This process involves:

- analysing the job requirements
- attracting employees to the job
- screening and selecting applicants
- hiring the successful candidate
- providing the new candidate with induction into the organisation.

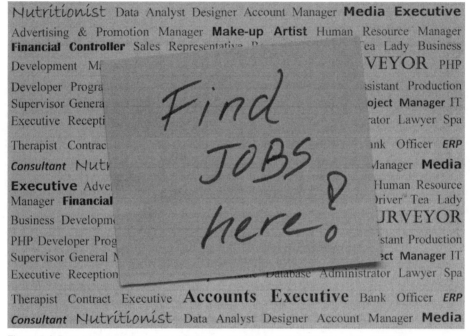

Figure 5.4 Recruitment is the process of finding a candidate to fill a position in an organisation.

Recruitment policy

All organisations will have a recruitment policy that outlines the organisation's recruitment process. The recruitment policy will be influenced by the organisational

> **DEFINITION**
>
> **interview** – a two-way communication between an interviewer and an applicant about a position at an organisation

culture of the business, which will influence which candidates will be attracted to the organisation. In South Africa, organisations also need to incorporate their own **affirmative action** targets.

Typically, a recruitment policy will consist of:
- a job analysis process (finding the need to fill a position)
- the job description guidelines
- the job specification guidelines
- the internal recruitment processes
- the criteria to follow to advertise the position externally
- the application processes
- the shortlisting guidelines
- the interview options
- the selection of candidates
- making the offer to the successful candidate
- the induction programme guidelines for new employees.

Recruitment sources

A company could recruit from within or from outside the organisation.

Internal recruitment
A business may decide to fill a vacancy from the existing staff within the organisation. Vacancies could be posted on office notice boards, on the intranet, in circulars, or internal newsletters. Potential candidates within the company can also be listed based on proven abilities in their existing positions.

There are many advantages of using internal recruitment:
- The candidates already know the organisation's policies and procedures.
- The candidates understand the organisational culture and will not need induction.
- It is more cost effective to fill a vacancy from existing staff.
- The position can be used as a promotion opportunity for a deserving candidate.
- The process of filling a vacancy is much quicker than when advertising for staff externally.
- Internal recruitment is a way to keep good employees.
- Internal recruitment reduces the risk of appointing the wrong person into a position.

External recruitment
For assorted reasons, the organisation may decide to find a suitable candidate using external sources. The organisation could advertise the position using:
- the internet (own website, other websites, or social media)
- newspaper, radio, and television advertisements.

DEFINITION

affirmative action – the policy of giving jobs and other opportunities to members of groups, such as racial minorities or women, who might not otherwise have them

---

The organisation could also recruit fresh staff through job recruitment agencies and educational institutions, or by personal endorsements of friends or family. In addition, the business could recruit staff from:

- competing companies (hiring someone who worked for a competitor)
- non-competing companies (hiring someone who worked for a supplier, service provider, or was a customer of the organisation).

A business could also:

- 'headhunt' candidates by searching recruiting websites like LinkedIn or Careers24.com for suitable candidates
- 'cold call' candidates who send in their CVs or contact information via diverse sources.

Figure 5.5 A business could 'cold call' candidates who send in their CVs.

Did you know? An organisation can advertise a position using an 'open advertisement' where all the organisation's information is provided, or by using a 'closed advertisement', where none of the organisation's information is shared.

Context and prescriptions

When planning its human resource provisioning, an organisation needs to consider that all employees in the organisation have basic human rights afforded to them by the South African Constitution 1996, Chapter 2: Bill of Rights, as well as the Universal Declaration of Human Rights drafted by the United Nations. The extract (shown below) from sections 9–14, 16 and 23 of Chapter 2 of the South African Constitution clearly show that all citizens have key rights (RSA, n.d.).

Section 9: Equality

3. The state may not unfairly discriminate directly or indirectly against anyone on one or more grounds, including race, gender, sex, pregnancy, marital status, ethnic or social origin, colour, sexual orientation, age, disability, religion, conscience, belief, culture, language and birth.

Section 10: Human dignity

Everyone has inherent dignity and the right to have their dignity respected and protected.

Section 11: Life

Everyone has the right to life.

Section 12: Freedom and security of the person

1. Everyone has the right to freedom and security of the person, which includes the right
   a. not to be deprived of freedom arbitrarily or without just cause;
   b. not to be detained without trial;
   c. to be free from all forms of violence from either public or private sources;
   d. not to be tortured in any way; and
   e. not to be treated or punished in a cruel, inhuman or degrading way.
2. Everyone has the right to bodily and psychological integrity, which includes the right
   a. to make decisions concerning reproduction;
   b. to security in and control over their body; and
   c. not to be subjected to medical or scientific experiments without their informed consent.

Section 13: Slavery, servitude and forced labour

No one may be subjected to slavery, servitude and forced labour.

Section 14: Privacy

Everyone has the right to privacy including the rights not to have:
   a. their person or home searched;
   b. their property searched;
   c. their possessions seized; or
   d. the privacy of their communication infringed.

Section 16: Freedom of expression

1. Everyone has the right to freedom of expression which includes:
   a. freedom of the press and other media;
   b. freedom to receive and impart information and ideas;
   c. freedom of artistic creativity;
   d. academic freedom and freedom of scientific research.

Section 23: Labour relations

1. Everyone has the right to fair labour practices.
2. Every worker has the right
   a. to form and join a trade union;
   b. to take part in the activities and programmes of a trade union; and
   c. to strike.
3. Every employer has the right
   a. to form and join an employers' organisation; and
   b. to take part in the activities and programmes of an employers' organisation.

4. Every trade union and every employers' organisation have the right
   a. to decide its own administration, programmes and activities;
   b. to organise; and
   c. to form and join a federation.
5. Every trade union, employers' organisation and employer have the right to engage in collective bargaining.

Discrimination

The Constitution makes it clear that the citizens of the country may not be discriminated against, especially in the workplace. These rights should be reflected in the recruitment policy and labour practices in the organisation.

This includes:

- advertisements that the organisation publishes or broadcasts
- interviews conducted with employees
- selection of suitable candidates whether from an internal or external source.

5.2.2 Paper selection of applicants

The selection process involves assessing all applications and finding candidates that are most suited to the position that needs to be filled. Those candidates are then invited to interviews to further refine the selection.

As the first step in finding new employment, prospective employees will complete two important forms/documents: an employment application form and a curriculum vitae (CV).

Employment application form

The completed employment application form is the first screening tool in the selection process. The main purpose of the form is to collect the personal information and relevant information about each candidate. Management uses the information to compare candidates using the same criteria and to prepare for the interviews with the candidates.

Figure 5.6 An employment application form is the first screening tool in the selection process.

Format of the application form

The application form should include sections for:

- personal information
- job specification information
- educational qualifications
- earlier work experience
- job-specific questions (optional)
- job references.

Advantages

These are some of the advantages of using employment application forms:

- Candidate information is provided in a consistent manner. This makes it easier to compare applicants.
- The manager can use the application form as a guide when preparing for an interview.
- The application form can be used as a selection tool to find suitable candidates.

Disadvantages

There are also disadvantages of using employment application forms:

- They add an added administrative burden on the human resources department and the recruiting manager.
- Information in the application form is a duplication of effort as the candidate will probably give the same information in the CV.
- It may take time and effort to design a suitable application form, especially if the position needs to be filled urgently.
- An application form can give insufficient information on candidates if the form has not been designed properly.
- The manager can also make over-hasty judgements of applicants based on the information provided, for example, a good worker could be overlooked due to an untidy application form.

Curriculum vitae

As part of the application process, organisations require applicants to send a curriculum vitae. A CV gives a summary of the applicant's professional experience, educational background, and other relevant information.

There are many good examples of a CV layout on the internet

The importance of a CV

A good CV helps to make a good first impression on a potential employer. It provides the employer with the relevant information about the applicant and could lead to an opportunity for an interview. A good CV should be no longer than two pages.

The layout of a CV

A CV should have the following sections:

- Personal details – name, surname, address, and contact numbers
- Personal profile – summary of areas of expertise and characteristics
- Key skills – explanation of the candidate's personal skills

- Education and qualifications – the candidate's school, college and university qualifications and achievements
- Employment history – starting with the candidate's current position and working backwards
- Hobbies and interests – this shows the candidate's personality
- References – key contacts that the applicant provides to give an account of the applicant

5.2.3 Procedures and documents used in the final stages before the appointment

After receiving all the application forms and CVs from the applicants, the manager and human resources will start the selection process. Human resources will then:

- screen through all the CVs and applications, then select the candidates that meet the minimum requirements for the position (shortlist).
- conduct background checks on the candidates
- undertake testing and evaluation of the candidates
- arrange for medical examinations of the candidates
- obtain security clearances on the candidates.

Verification of candidates' background

The background checks include checking whether the candidates' qualifications and other information given on the CVs and application forms are valid. It also entails contacting the candidates' reference/s to get more information about them.

Testing and evaluation

Some organisations require candidates to do a selection test before or after an interview. In most cases, the test is to assess whether the candidates will be able to deal with some of the work that they will have to do in the new position. The tests could include **psychometric tests**.

> **Did you know?** Psychometric tests are only allowed if they are fair to all employees – refer to Section 8 of the Employment Equity Act (No. 55 of 1998).

> **DEFINITION**
>
> **psychometric test –** used to assess whether someone has the right aptitude, attitude, behaviour, intelligence, and other qualities needed to do a job

Figure 5.7 A candidate is usually given a medical examination.

Medical examination

Generally, a medical examination is reserved for the successful candidate before starting in the new position. However, organisations can ask that all short-listed candidates do medical examinations to determine whether they are emotionally and physically fit enough to perform the job.

Security clearance

With the increase in white-collar crime, many organisations have added security clearance checks to their recruitment policy. These security clearances show whether the candidate has a criminal record or poor credit rating, which could show a possible weakness to temptation, especially when working with cash or finances.

5.2.4 Interviewing applicants

Following the short-listing and background checks of the candidates, the next phase of recruitment is the applicant's interview. This gives the manager and HR an opportunity to assess whether any of the short-listed candidates are best suited for the position.

Arrangements prior to the interview

On the day of the interview, the secretary/management assistant will ensure that all the necessary arrangements have been put in place. These include confirming that:
- the meeting room (away from all the noise) has been booked
- the panellists and candidates have been told of the time of the interview(s).

In addition, the secretary/management assistant must ensure that the interview room is properly prepared and that there is comfortable seating for all and that there are no telephones. Other staff members must be reminded not to disturb the interviews taking place.

Preparation by the interviewer

To make the most of the interview process, the interviewer must be properly prepared. To help with this preparation, the interviewer should:

- review and understand the job analysis that was conducted
- review the job description and job specifications
- be familiar with the recruitment policy of the organisation
- review all short-listed candidates' CVs, application forms and background information
- prepare a list of questions that they would like the candidates to answer
- arrive with the candidates' interview files with all supporting documents.

Files needed for the interviews

To prepare for the interviews, the interviewer puts together a file for each candidate having:

- the applicant's CV
- the applicant's completed application form
- a report on the person's background checks
- the results of testing (psychometric/selection).

The interview process

During the interview, the interviewer should:

- discuss the key requirements of the job
- discuss the salary and fringe benefits that the organisation gives
- go through the information provided in the application form and CV
- find out why the applicant applied for the position
- ask questions related to situations that could be met in the job to assess the candidate's response to each scenario
- allow the applicant to ask questions about the job, salary, fringe benefits and the organisation.

During the interview, the interviewer must keep notes on the candidates' responses, both verbally and non-verbally. The interviewer must also listen attentively during the interview and show a genuine interest in the applicant's answers to questions.

Figure 5.8 The interviewer should show a genuine interest in the applicant's answers to questions.

During the interviews, the interviewer(s) should keep a score on each candidate to help with the final decision about the selection.

The organisation could decide to have a second round of interviews. These interviews may include only two or three candidates. The second interview could be a panel interview where the candidates face questions from different interviewers. The panellists will combine their assessments of the candidates to reach a decision of who to appoint in the position.

5.2.5 Types of interviews

Table 5.2 explains several types of interviews that an organisation may use.

Table 5.2 Types of interviews

Type of interview	Description
Structured (standardised) interview	In a structured interview, the interviewer is experienced and asks a pre-determined set of questions to all candidates. This is a formal and inflexible type of interview. This is also known as an in-depth interview. Candidates will mainly answer 'Yes' or 'No'.
Unstructured interview	The interviewer does not need to be experienced and asks open-ended questions. The interview is less formal and is more flexible. The candidate is free to answer the questions. These interviews take much longer due to the freedom granted in answering the questions.
Stress interview	This type of interview is also known as a tension/pressure interview. These interviews are designed to test a candidate's ability to think on their feet. Questions are asked randomly and mainly try to put the candidate under pressure to see the reaction. These interviews may involve using unfair criticism, interruptions, or silence to create a pressure situation. This technique is typically used for sales type jobs as these applicants may be faced with more pressure situations when selling a product or a service.
Panel interview	A panel interview is an interview where there are several interviewers present. Each panellist is given an opportunity to ask the candidate questions. This type of interview is popular in educational institutions, where the panel may include the principal, the chairperson of the governing body, an educator's representative, and a student representative.

Figure 5.9 A secretary in a panel interview

5.2.6 Characteristics of the interviewer

All interviewers should have the following characteristics:

- They must be good listeners.
- They should be professional in the manner that they conduct themselves.
- They should keep eye contact with the candidates and be confident enough to ask intelligent questions.
- They should be polite and help nervous candidates to calm down.
- They should make notes while the candidates answer the questions.
- They should be objective in evaluating candidates.
- They should articulate questions clearly and not make it too complicated for the candidates.
- They should be good ambassadors for the organisation.
- They should have enough experience in the organisation to be able to answer questions about the organisation.
- They should have a sound knowledge of the salary and fringe benefits offered in the position.

5.2.7 Do's and don'ts of interviews

There are certain things that both the interviewer and candidate can do to make sure that the interview is successful, which will be an advantage to the enterprise.

- Both the interviewer and candidate should be well prepared for the interview.
- The interview should be done in a systematic fashion and not be a tense occasion.
- The interviewer should try to gather the relevant information about the candidate.

- There should be no interruptions or disruptions during the interview.
- The interviewer must still be focused and listen attentively to the candidate.
- The candidate's file with all supporting documents should be available at the start of the interview.
- Both interviewer and candidate should be on time for the interview.
- Neither interviewer or candidate should leave the meeting before the end of the interview.
- Neither the interviewer or candidate should be distracted, even when someone else is asking questions.
- The interviewer should not interrupt the candidate when talking.

5.2.8 Pitfalls that result in an unsuccessful interview

There are many pitfalls that result in an unsuccessful interview. This could result from the following:
- The interviewer speaks too much, and the candidate only answers 'Yes' or 'No'.
- The interviewer is not prepared for the interview.
- The candidates are not properly screened or the interview file is not up-to-date.
- The venue for the interview is too noisy and causes many distractions.
- The candidate is overcome by nervousness and does not answer the questions correctly.
- The interviewer does not understand the requirements of the job.
- The interviewer selects the candidate on a 'gut feel'.
- None of the short-listed candidates is suitable for the position.

Power break 5.2   INDIVIDUAL WORK

Find all the discriminatory aspects in the advertisement and show why it is discriminatory.

TEACHING OPPORTUNITIES ABROARD

A well-established international school abroad is looking for dynamic, enthusiastic teaching professionals to join a successful team. A young white female between 25–35 years old, who is positive, with excellent classroom practices, is needed.

Forward your CV, a letter of application, contact details and a recent photograph.

Requirements:
- Bachelor of Education degree*
- Minimum of 5 years' experience

*Note: Distance learning qualifications are not accepted in our country.

UNIT 5.3 **Selection and appointment**

This unit focuses on the actual selection and appointment of a successful new employee.

5.3.1 Selection policy and procedure

The main aim of a selection policy is to ensure that a thorough and open process is followed for all appointments in the organisation. The policy also ensures that the final selection and appointment is based on the candidate's skills, knowledge, aptitude, attitude, personality, and other relevant criteria.

5.3.2 Selection process

The selection of the successful candidate begins during the interviews. The selection process is as follows.

- During the interviews, the interviewer/panellists will make notes about each short-listed candidate and give a score to each of them.
- Once these scores are added and the preferred candidate found, the manager will tell HR to prepare the written offer to be sent to the new employee.
- The manager can set up a meeting with the candidate to go through the **written offer** and allow the candidate to sign it.
- The manager could also email the offer to the candidate for signature. In this case, the candidate needs to sign the offer and return it to either the recruiting manager or the HR department before the set deadline.
- The manager and the candidate need to agree on a starting date for the position, as the **incumbent** may need to give notice to their current employer before starting the new job.
- When the signed offer is received, the HR department will open a new employee number in the payroll system and start adding the benefits as stipulated in the written offer.
- HR will also tell the IT department to prepare the new employee's computer and create a new email address for them.

Figure 5.10 A new employee will be given a workstation.

> **DEFINITIONS**
>
> **written offer** – this offer includes the salary, pension/provident fund, medical aid, leave and other benefits that the employee will receive
>
> **incumbent** – the person now in a position

- The recruiting manager must ensure that the new employee has a workstation given and that all the necessary connections, for example, computer, modem, and telephone, are in place and working.
- HR will tell switchboard of the new employee's workstation and telephone extension number.
- HR must tell security to create a new access card and parking access (if available) for the new employee.
- HR will also schedule the new employee's induction and confirm with those involved in the programme to prepare for the new employee's arrival.
- HR will tell the finance department of the new appointment and ensure that all relevant information is added to the accounting system.

5.3.3 Equal employment opportunities

To address the injustices of the apartheid system, the South African government introduced the affirmative action policy (Employment Equity Act, 55 of 1998) which requires organisations to give preference to designated groups (black, coloured, Indian, women and the disabled) when making appointments in the organisation. The organisation needs to set an employment equity target for the organisation and report on their appointments during the year.

5.3.4 Placing the correct person in a post

Throughout the recruitment and selection process, the organisation works toward appointing the correct and best-suited person to a post. The best-suited candidate will emerge from the list of candidates who have applied for a position. The success of the selection comes from proper job analysis, job description, job specification, advertising, short-listing, interviewing and final selection.

5.3.5 Appointment

The culmination of the selection process is when the manager makes a firm offer to the selected candidate to join the organisation. The written offer is a summary of the service contract that the new employee will sign, either with the written offer or when starting in the new position.

Acceptance by the applicant

In the offer letter sent/given to the applicant, there would be a section that the applicant must sign to accept the offer that has been made. The signed acceptance of the offer must then be given back to the manager and/or HR to confirm the appointment. Once received, the signed acceptance starts the process of creating a new employee in the payroll system and other relevant systems.

Psychological contract

A psychological contract is an implied or **tacit** agreement between employer and employee about the mutual obligations towards each other. It sets out what a new employee's expectations are in terms of salary, leave and other benefits that are provided with the acceptance of the offer. The organisation also has similar expectations that the employee will perform the work needed at an acceptable level.

Service contract

A service contract is a formal agreement between the employee and the organisation. The contract will have information relating to:

- any **probationary** period
- the contract start and end dates (if applicable)
- hours of work and overtime
- salary
- the pension/provident fund and medical aid
- absence from work
- leave (annual, study, sick, family responsibility and maternity)
- confidentiality in the workplace
- company disciplinary procedures
- retrenchment procedures
- termination of service.

Figure 5.11 Signing a service contract.

Power break 5.3   INDIVIDUAL WORK

To ensure a fair and effective appointment you were asked to put together a selection procedure for your organisation. Make use of the following headings and explain in each one what process will be followed.

1   Physical and psychometric testing
2   Reference checking
3   Application form
4   Successful candidate appointed
5   Review and evaluate CVs and interviews

UNIT 5.4   Induction

When a new employee starts at an organisation, it is important to properly induct the employee into the organisation and give them an overview of how the organisation functions.

5.4.1 Importance of an induction programme

The induction programme aims to orientate a new employee into the organisation. The programme typically covers:

- the organisation's vision, mission, goals, and objectives
- the history of the organisation
- the organisation's policies and procedures
- the organisational and reporting structure in the organisation
- the departments within the organisation and what each department does
- a meeting with the departmental heads to gain an insight about the functioning of each department
- the organisation's products and/or services
- the key markets in which the organisation operates and the organisation's main customers
- the basics of logging on to the organisation's computer network
- the personnel expenditure claims procedure
- an introduction to the office staff
- contracts and other documents that the employee will be expected to work with
- an overview of the office layout and where the working areas, kitchen and toilets are found.

Figure 5.12 During an induction programme, new staff are introduced to their colleagues in the business.

5.4.2 Follow-up after induction programme

An induction programme can be very overwhelming to a new employee, and there should be a follow-up with the new employee after the induction. This follow-up could be done by a combination of the following activities:

- The company can appoint a **mentor** to look after the new employee. The mentor should regularly check that the new employee has settled in at the organisation.
- The employee's manager can confirm whether the employee has settled in and check if the new staff member needs any guidance about what was covered in the induction programme.
- HR can send the employee a copy of any presentations used in the induction programme. This will allow the employee to refer to the material if needed.
- HR can follow up with the employee after a few days to confirm that the employee has no problems and is settling in well in the new job.
- The manager can schedule monthly/weekly meetings with the employee to see if there are any areas of concern that the employee may have within the new organisation.
- A review form can be sent to the employee after the induction to rate the various aspects of the induction programme.

Power break 5.4   INDIVIDUAL WORK

As a senior secretarial assistant, you were instructed by your manager to draw up an induction programme for the new junior secretary. The induction programme should include the following information: Policy, contracts, processes, introduction to colleagues, facilities, other departments and work stations. Indicate who handles each item.

DEFINITION

mentor – a person who gives a younger or less experienced person help and advice over a period, especially at work or school

UNIT 5.5 Human resources training and development

All employees, irrespective of the number of years in any given job, will at some stage need training and/or personal development to overcome any weaknesses they or management may have found.

5.5.1 Training of secretarial staff

Effective training and development is important to ensure that a secretary/management assistant has a sound knowledge of the many various aspects of the work involved within the secretarial field. The need for training stems from the self-actualisation needs as given in Maslow's hierarchy of needs.

Table 5.3 details the main aims of training.

Table 5.3 The main aims of training

Aims of training	Explanation
Increase productivity	Training teaches employees better ways of doing certain activities. This will increase their productivity.
Improve morale	Training helps employees feel that they have learned new skills or behaviours. This will boost their morale.
Lower the staff turnover	When employees realise that the organisation is willing to spend money on training them, they tend to be more loyal to the business and will not leave as easily.
Improve client or customer relations	With improved skills and behaviours, employees will offer the organisation's customers or clients a better service.
Improve time and resource management	New skills and behaviours will help employees use their time and resources more productively.
Increase promotion possibilities	Training will give employees new skills and behaviours. This will lead to more promotion opportunities.
Keep abreast of advances in technology	Training will ensure that employees keep up-to-date with ongoing changes in technology that affect the organisation. This will make the employee more effective in the workplace.

5.5.2 Steps in the training process

Table 5.4 shows the steps in the training process.

Table 5.4 Steps in the training process

Serial	Step in the process	Description
1	Determine the training needs	Training programmes are based on a needs audit within the organisation.
2	Define the objective of training.	Having found the training needs, the objective of the training should be to satisfy the training needs.
3	Find the target audience.	By looking at the training needs of all employees, a list of attendees can be drawn up.
4	Decide on the training method.	The organisation must assess which training method (classroom-based, computer-based, or on-the-job training) will be used to train staff.
5	Decide on centralised or decentralised training.	Management will decide whether to train all the delegates at a central location or in various locations.
6	Define the content of the training programme.	Once the needs have been found, the location decided, and the training method defined, the organisation must decide on the content to be included in the training programme.
7	Complete the training.	To get the most benefits from training, the training must be completed within an agreed timeframe.
8	Post-training evaluation	After the training, the participants can either complete a test or a questionnaire where they can rate the effectiveness of the training and give feedback on ways to improve the programme for future training sessions.

5.5.3 Difference between training and development

The following table summarises the key differences between training and development.

Table 5.5 The differences between training and development

Training	Development
Training teaches a new skill, behaviour or ability that is needed to do a job.	Development is a process aimed at improving an employee's capabilities for promotion in the organisation.
Training is task focused.	Development helps to develop an employee's potential.
Successful training depends on the skills of the trainer.	Successful development is dependent on the individual employee.
Training is a short-term event.	Development is an ongoing process.

5.5.4 Training methods and opportunities

An organisation can use different training methods to address the training needs of a secretary/management assistant and other staff members.

In-service training

Employees receive in-service training as and when new skills and abilities are needed. This training is mainly concerned with learning policies and procedures that are unique to the organisation.

Short courses (internal and external)

A short course is focused on a specific topic, such as a new email programme that the organisation is implementing. The trainer can be from within the organisation or could be an expert from outside the organisation.

Formal training

A formal training course is run by a skilled trainer. Employees normally receive certificates to acknowledge that they completed the course.

Job rotation

With job rotation, employees get the opportunity to do different jobs for certain periods to get a better understanding of each job. Job rotation is normally used to prepare employees for senior positions and helps them to understand the distinct types of work and procedures these more senior positions entail.

Mentoring/role model

Mentoring is a programme where senior staff members are given junior staff members to mentor. The mentors will meet with the new employees on a regular basis and help them with issues that they may be struggling with in the workplace.

Selective reading list

Selective reading lists are especially useful to keep abreast with new technological advances and other developments that could affect the organisation. The responsible employee will study the required reading material and either compile a book review or give a presentation of the information to staff who may be affected by the changes/advances.

In-basket or role play

An in-basket activity involves a manager or colleague showing a new employee what actions need to be taken with each document that arrives in an in-basket. A role play involves two or more employees playing different roles to simulate a scenario that they may meet in the job.

Case studies

A case study involves using a simulation situation to try to find solutions for problems given in the simulation.

Management games

Management games can be used to train potential managers on how to make effective decisions, deal with problems and determine priorities. There are numerous management games available for download from the internet.

Syndicate training

Syndicate training is where employees are divided into groups and each group has tasks that they must do. All the team members must be actively involved in the training.

Computer-based training

The World Wide Web has radically changed the picture of training. Programs such as YouTube carry many training videos that can be accessed from anywhere in the world with an internet connection. A secretary/management assistant can access this material any time to help improve specific skills, abilities or behaviours. Some companies have training centres that do large-scale computer-based training.

Figure 5.13 Some companies have training centres that do large-scale computer-based training.

Audio, audio-visual aids in training

Trainers usually use audio and visual aids during training sessions. When using visual aids, such as slides, transparencies, charts and graphs, trainers should:
- keep presentations short and make content easy to read
- make use of colour and animations to make the content interesting
- keep in mind that the audience must be able to see and hear the presentation clearly
- test and set up the presentations before the meeting/conference begins.

When using audio aids, such as a radio or tape recorder, trainers should:
- make sure that the speakers are in good working order and cover the entire meeting room
- use only high-quality recordings
- use proper language and clear pronunciation
- ensure that the material is at the right starting point to avoid unnecessary delays.

When using audio-visual aids, such as television, films and videos, trainers should:
- ensure that the picture quality is of a high standard and can be seen from all parts of the venue
- ensure that the sound quality is good and can be clearly heard by all participants at the venue
- ensure that the videos are at the correct starting point to avoid delays
- keep the videos short to keep the audience's attention
- manage the lighting so that the picture is not affected. Close the blinds and make the room dark if necessary.

5.5.5 Evaluation of internal training

Once the secretary/management assistant or other staff member has attended a training programme, it is important to evaluate the training. The main aims of such an evaluation are:
- to find out whether the training met with the pre-training expectations of the trainee
- to assess whether the content of the programme was enough to address the training needs of the trainee
- to evaluate whether the trainer was able to reach all the participants in the training
- to decide whether the venue used was adequate for the training group
- to assess whether the training material given was suitable
- to give the trainees an opportunity to give recommendations on how to improve the training for the next training group.

5.5.6 Requirements of evaluation instruments

Evaluation instruments help decide whether an applicant will perfectly fit the job or not. These evaluation instruments include tests and questionnaires and should meet the following requirements:

- Reliability – it must give the same results if used continually.
- Validity – it must measure the right skills needed in the job.
- Objective – the evaluation can be used for all the participants.
- Degree of difficulty – by giving different levels of difficulty it can help participants' growth and development
- The test must be set up, conducted, and interpreted by knowledgeable people

5.5.7 System for storing and safekeeping of training material

All training material should be stored in a resource library for future reference. For ease of access, this library can be within the secretary/management assistant's work area or in a central work area. The training material should be correctly labelled and filed in a logical manner. Audio and visual training material should be kept in a protective case/sleeve to prevent damage from dust and other contaminants.

5.5.8 Career path planning

This last section discusses the important aspect of career path planning. Reflect back to Module 1, Figure 1.13, which shows the promotion route of a secretarial career. This diagram will help the manager to develop a clear action plan to ensure that the secretary/management assistant can make the necessary progression and move up the various levels of the promotion route/career path. This is done by setting short-, medium- and long-term plans incorporating both training and development activities.

Power break 5.5   INDIVIDUAL WORK

When would the company make use of the following types of in-service training methods?

Type of training	When to use
1. Coaching	
2. Work rotation	

continued on next page …

Power break 5.5 INDIVIDUAL WORK

Type of training	When to use
3. Internship	
4. Mentoring	
5. Task instruction	
6. Computer based training	

WHAT DO WE KNOW AND WHERE TO NEXT?

This module discussed staffing, recruitment, and interviewing. We then covered selection and appointment followed by induction. We ended the module with an in-depth study of human resource training and development

The next module considers aspects of human resource maintenance and administration.

Revisiting the learning objectives

Now that you have completed this module you should have achieved the learning objectives listed in the table below.

Learning objective	What you have learned	✔
Explain human resources planning.	Human resource planning involves: • doing the job analysis • defining the job specification and job description • using job enrichment and job enhancement techniques.	☐
Explain recruitment as an important function of human resources provisioning.	In human resource provisioning, recruitment brings the job analysis to life as a business policy on recruitment in put in place. This is followed by recruitment from internal or external recruitment sources. Recruitment must be understood within the South African context and should avoid being discriminatory.	☐
Explain paper selection of applicants (in order to compile a shortlist).	Once the recruitment process has been completed, the manager and human resources will do a paper selection of the most suitable candidates that are short-listed. This involves reviewing application forms, and curriculum vitae (CVs).	☐
Explain the procedures and documentation used in the final stage before the appointment of new staff.	Following the short-listing of the candidates, the verification of background information, testing and evaluation, medical examination and security clearances are completed.	☐

continued on next page ...

Learning objective	What you have learned	✔
Explain interviewing of applicants for a vacant post.	After all the checks have been completed, the candidates can be interviewed. This entails creating a file for each applicant, which includes: • application form • CV • background report • results of testing • results of medical examination • other documents as needed • the list of the fringe benefits and services given by the undertaking. There are several types of interviews that can be used including: • structured interviews • unstructured interviews • stress interviews • panel interviews.	☐
	The interview is conducted in a room away from noise with no telephone interruptions, comfortable chairs, and no disturbance by staff members.	☐
After having viewed a video on an interview for a post, find the advantages of a successful interview, the pitfalls, and problems of a poorly conducted interview as well as the do's and don'ts concerning interviews.	A successful interview is characterised by both candidate and interviewer being well prepared, the interviewer working systematically and the interviewer gathering the right information from the candidate, keeping to the dos and the don'ts of interviews and avoiding the pitfalls of a poorly conducted interview.	☐
Briefly elucidate on the selection policy appointment and procedure about human resource management.	The selection policy of the organisation shows a thorough and transparent process was followed and the candidate was selected based on skills, knowledge, aptitude, attitude, personality, etc.	☐
Briefly explain equal employment opportunities and affirmative action as components of a selection policy for human resource management.	Equal employment opportunities in South Africa were introduced to favour designated groups (blacks, coloureds, Indians, female and disabled). Organisations set affirmative action targets and are assessed to see if they have met these targets.	☐
Elucidate on the necessity of the correct placement of the correct person in a particular post.	Selecting the best suited candidate in a position helps the organisation be more productive and effective. This helps the organisation to move closer to achieving its organisational goals and objectives.	☐

continued on next page …

Learning objective	What you have learned	✔
Explain the appointment of a successful applicant:	A successful applicant is made a written offer, which is a summary of the service contract that the employee will sign before starting in the new position.	☐
Explain the importance of an induction programme for newly appointed staff for both the organisation and the employee.	An induction programme will help a new employee to understand the organisation better and see how it differs from all others. The programme should cover the organisation's history, products/services, organisational structure, departmental functions, IT systems and introduction to colleagues.	☐
Briefly explain why it is necessary to do a follow-up after the induction programme.	The follow-up after the induction ensures that the employee has settled into the new position and understands the ins and outs of the organisation.	☐
Explain training of secretarial staff (secretaries/ management assistants and support staff).	Training secretarial staff starts with understanding the aims of training, the necessity for personal development to cope with technological advancements. Opportunities for training include in-service training, short courses, formal training.	☐
Briefly explain the difference between training and development.	Training teaches new skills, behaviour or ability that is needed to do a job.

Development is a process aimed at improving the person's capabilities for promotion in the organisation. | ☐ |
| Explain development programmes/ techniques for secretaries/ management assistants. | To help a secretary/management assistant to move from a Level 1 position to the top-tier (Level 4) position, the manager/supervisor should use:
• job rotation
• mentoring
• selective reading list
• In-basket or role play. | ☐ |

Assessment

1. Multiple choice

Choose the correct answers from the various options provided. Choose A, B, C or D and write it next to the question number.

1.1 _____ is one of the in-service training and development methods.

    A   In-basket

    B   Syndicate training

    C   Coaching

    D   Role play

1.2 Which of the following is an example of a recruitment media?

    A   pamphlet

    B   radio

    C   brochure

    D   all the above

1.3 A _____ is also called an in-depth interview.

    A   walk-in interview

    B   standardised interview

    C   structured interview

    D   panel interview

1.4 _____ is the type of interview where an openly hostile attitude is taken towards the applicant by the panel.

    A   An open/unstructured interview

    B   A stress interview

    C   A panel interview

    D   A structured interview

1.5 A process where vacancies are filled within the company is called _____.

    A   internal recruitment

    B   selection

    C   external recruitment

    D   recruitment

(5 × 1 = 5)

[5]

2. True or false

Choose whether the following statements are true or false. Write down the number of the question and 'true' or 'false'.

2.1 A follow-up process in the induction process is when the head of the department regularly contacts the new employee.

2.2 Advertising is an example of an internal recruitment resource.

2.3 It is necessary to appoint the right person to avoid absence from work.

2.4 Staffing is the selection and training of individuals for specific job functions and making them responsible to perform those job functions.

2.5 An interview is one-way communication from the candidate to the interviewer.

(5 × 1 = 5)

[5]

3. Match the columns

Choose a description from Column B that matches the word/item in Column A. Write only the letter (A–E) next to the question number.

Column A	Column B
3.1 Recruitment	A. This entails introducing a new worker to the new work environment.
3.2 Personnel provisioning	B. This supplements the application form.
3.3 Curriculum vitae (CV)	C. This entails all activities involved in finding a suitable candidate for the job.
3.4 Labour bureaus	D. Human resource planning goes hand-in-hand with _____.
3.5 Induction	E. This Is not a recruitment media.

(5 × 2 = 10)

[10]

4. Short questions

Give a short description of the following terms:

4.1 selection

4.2 job analysis

4.3 security clearance

4.4 service contract

4.5 development

(5 × 2 = 10)

[10]

5. Long questions

5.1 Most organisations give training away from the workplace during team-building sessions. The main idea is to strengthen relationships amongst colleagues. Discuss the techniques applied when training employees away from work. (20)

5.2 Businesses use tests and questionnaires to judge an applicant's abilities objectively. They help in deciding whether the applicant will perfectly fit the job or not. Discuss five requirements with which evaluation instruments (like tests and questionnaires) need to comply. (5 × 2 = 10)

[30]

6. Case study

Read this example of a selection policy and answer the questions that follow.

A selection policy

Attract and retain high calibre employees who are suitably qualified to:

- perform the inherent requirements of the job
- facilitate effective and efficient recruitment and selection
- align recruitment and selection practices with all legal and ethical requirements.

Ensure that recruitment and selection decisions take objective criteria into account and that procedures are fair.

Promote equal opportunity in the workplace by eliminating unfair discrimination and facilitate the equitable representation of Africans, Indians, coloureds, women, and people with disabilities ('designated groups') in all occupational categories and levels in the workforce through promoting the objectives of the municipality's employment equity policy.

6.1 Discuss five aspects/questions a policy should address during the selection process. (5 × 2 = 10)

6.2 'When recruiting new employees an organisation's advertising should not be discriminatory.'

Create a short job advertisement for a junior secretary and ensure that it is not discriminatory. (5 × 2 = 10)

[20]

Grand total: 80 marks

HUMAN RESOURCES MAINTENANCE AND ADMINISTRATION

This module considers the following aspects of human resources maintenance and administration:

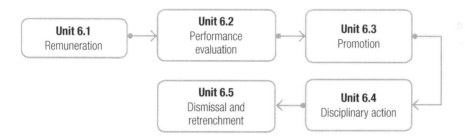

Learning objectives

After completing this module, you should be able to do the following:

- Explain human resources planning.
- Briefly explain the remuneration of staff.
- Explain the aims and methods of performance evaluation in general and elucidate on how performance evaluation could be carried out for junior secretaries and secretaries/management assistants.
- Elucidate on the promotion of staff.
- Explain disciplinary action.
- Explain in detail the procedure to be followed when disciplinary action is taken against an employee.
- Differentiate between dismissal, retrenchment, lay-off and retirement of staff.
- Explain in detail the process of dismissal of an employee, also stating the requirements according to policy, law and labour unions.

Key terms

arbitrator	peers	remuneration
consultation	performance evaluation	retrenchment
corrective sanction	procedurally fair	subordinates
disciplinary action	punitive sanction	substantively fair
dismissal	redundancy	

Starting point

Verushna has discovered the joys of starting a new job have their rewards, such as earning a regular income in the form of remuneration (salary or wages). All workers within the organisation will strive to meet their individual needs and help the organisation achieve its goals and objectives. The organisation tracks the performance of the employees by doing performance evaluations that aim to highlight which workers are top performers in the organisation, and to pinpoint employees that need support to improve their productivity. This provides the organisation with information on which employees are ready to be moved into management and which employees can be moved to various parts of the organisation to gain experience in other environments.

Unfortunately, Verushna also found out that there are also situations where employees do not follow the organisation's disciplinary code and are subjected to disciplinary action. Similarly, employees may raise grievances that need to be addressed by management.

Figure 6.1 Verushna's colleagues have shown her that starting a new job has its rewards.

UNIT 6.1 **Remuneration**

The day you receive your first wages or salary is a very proud moment. If you have studied and successfully completed your qualification, it makes the moment even more special. This module discusses how that first pay cheque is structured.

6.1.1 Direct remuneration

Direct **remuneration** is a payment received for work that someone has completed. You are paid for the hours that you have worked or are paid a commission (percentage of the total sales price) on the sales that you made. This money is paid either monthly, weekly, or even on an event happening (completing a sale). Table 6.1 shows the components that could be included in direct remuneration.

Table 6.1 Components of direct remuneration

Component	Description
Gross salary	The salary before deductions.
Commission	An amount normally paid to sales staff and usually based on a percentage of the total sales.
Bonus	An incentive amount paid to an employee, either annually or for achieving a special target.
Overtime	An amount paid to employees who have worked more than the standard number of working hours for the week/month. The Basic Conditions of Employment Act of 1998 stipulates that this only applies if the person earns less than R144 000 per annum.
Income tax	The amount deducted from a salary and paid to the Receiver of Revenue (SARS). This is also referred to as PAYE (Pay-as-you-earn).
Pension contribution	An amount deducted from a salary. The employer will also contribute an amount This contribution is invested in a pension fund and is paid to the worker on retirement as a monthly sum.
Provident fund contribution	Like a pension fund scheme, except that a part (normally 1/3) is paid when the person retires. The balance is paid in monthly instalments.
Medical aid contribution:	The amount deducted from an employee's salary as a contribution to a medical aid scheme. This gives medical cover to the employee and the employee's family.
Unemployment insurance fund	An amount deducted from a salary to give funds in case the employee becomes unemployed.
Skills development levy	A deduction made from a salary that goes towards skills development (training).
Group life cover	Insurance cover is taken out on the life of the employee.
Net salary	The salary amount that is left over from the gross salary after all the deductions.

> **DEFINITION**
>
> **remuneration** – payment for work done

6.1.2 Indirect remuneration

Indirect remuneration is any benefits given to an employee over and above their direct remuneration. These are also called fringe benefits. Examples of fringe benefits include a housing subsidy, which is an amount that the organisation pays towards the employee's monthly bond repayments.

Employees are allowed several types of paid leave. These include:

- annual leave (also known as paid leave)
- maternity leave, which is leave taken during pregnancy; usually a period of four months
- paternity leave, which is leave taken by the father of a new born baby; usually only three days
- study leave, which is leave taken to study for and write an exam
- family responsibility leave, which is leave taken to care for a sick direct family member
- compassionate leave, which is leave taken after the death of a direct family member
- sick leave, which is leave taken due to ill health.

In addition, employees may be entitled to:

- low interest loans, which are loans given to an employee by an organisation at lower interest rate than is charged by commercial bank
- low or cheap prices, which is when staff can buy products or services from the organisation at a price below the regular selling price
- bursaries, which may be offered to employees or their direct family to cover for their tuition, books, equipment, accommodation and/or transport costs
- the use of company assets, when employees can use certain assets of the organisation, for example, a company car or cellphone
- a cellphone allowance, which an employee receives to cover personal cellphone costs
- a travel allowance, which is an amount paid to an employee for distance travelled for business purposes
- a meal allowance, which is an amount paid to an employee to cover costs of meals during business travels.

6.1.3 Salary scale

Organisations use specific salary scales to allow for differences in experience, qualifications, and work performance of employees in the same job category. The salary scale will give a higher salary to someone who has more experience, a higher qualification and is more productive than someone else. When graduates join an organisation, they would normally start at the bottom of the salary scale, however, with more experience and consistent work performance, they can steadily move up the scale.

Figure 6.2 With consistently good work performance, employees can move up the salary scale.

Did you know? Employers are allowing employees more flexibility in the way their salary is structured. They could offer the employee a 'total cost of employment salary' where the employee decides how much to contribute to each part of the salary. For example, an employee could decide to give 20% toward a pension and not pay for medical aid.

Power break 6.1   PAIR WORK

Work with a partner, read the scenario given and then answer the questions that follow.

You have successfully completed your N6 studies and Dr Lucian Harmse has offered you a position as a medical secretary. He is offering you a 'total cost of employment' package of R10 000 per month. You have the following options available to you.

* You can contribute either 7% or 10% to your pension fund.
* You can also contribute 5% to a medical aid.
* You qualify for a R200 cellphone allowance for you to use as needed.
* Your monthly income tax is R2 000.

1 Calculate what your net salary will be if you choose to contribute 10% toward your pension fund.
2 How much more would you take home if you decide to only contribute 7% to your pension?
3 In your opinion, which is a better choice for you as a young graduate? Motivate your answer.

UNIT 6.2 Performance evaluation

Performance evaluation is the process of reviewing the work performance of an employee against the targets that were set for the employee. A performance evaluation is also known as a performance appraisal.

6.2.1 Objectives of performance evaluation

Performance evaluation aims to assess the work performance of all employees. It will also:

- pinpoints employees' strengths, weaknesses, opportunities, and threats (SWOT)
- helps to assess training needs of employees
- shows leadership potential and individuals that can be placed in management
- rewards employees for excellent work performance
- gives grounds for job analysis that could lead to new positions in the organisation
- name areas where employees are overworked and not performing at the required standard
- encourages mediocre performers to work harder so that they can move into the top achiever category of performers.

6.2.2 Methods of performance evaluation

These are some of the methods used to evaluate the performance of an employee.

Self-evaluation

When doing a self-evaluation, an employee will make a list of their own performance. The manager can compare this self-assessment with the company's assessment of the employee's performance.

Bell curve

In a bell-curve performance evaluation, the employees are placed in a pool. Each employee's contribution to the overall organisational goals and aims is then assessed and ranked from highest to lowest in the pool. The results are plotted to show each employee's position on a graph.

> **DEFINITION**
>
> **performance evaluation** – the process of reviewing the work performance of an employee against the targets that were set for the employee

Figure 6.3 shows an example of a bell curve.

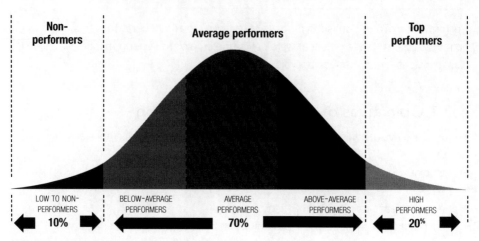

Figure 6.3 Bell curve used in performance appraisals.

Checklists

As an evaluation of performance, an employee can complete a checklist showing whether an activity was completed or not. Incomplete activities could show a developmental need and training may be needed to help the employee to complete the activities.

Observation

When using an observation method of evaluation, the employee's supervisor evaluates performance of a specific employee by observation and by comparing the performance with that of a peer employee.

Customer surveys

Customer surveys can provide valuable feedback on customers' interactions with

Figure 6.4 Managers can use a checklist to pinpoint employee training and developmental needs.

employees and can be used as a method of performance appraisal.

Critical incidents

A business can use reports on critical incidents to evaluate the good and bad aspects of an employee's performance.

360-degree evaluation

In a 360-degree evaluation, the employee's manager, other managers, the employee's **peers**, the employee's subordinates, and the employee's customers all give feedback on the employee's performance. The feedback is coordinated and used as a performance assessment tool.

Power break 6.2   INDIVIDUAL WORK

You are the executive secretary and you need to complete a performance evaluation on your junior secretary. Draw up a checklist of items that you would include in such an evaluation. Examples of items you could include are telephone skills, customer relations and filing.

UNIT 6.3 **Promotion**

Following on from the performance evaluation, managers could pinpoint employees who show the potential to be moved to the next level on their promotion route.

6.3.1 The difference between promotion and transfer

Promotion is moving to a higher rank in the organisation, with more responsibilities, increased salary and a higher status. For example, promotion from a junior secretary to senior secretary.

A transfer is sideways movement in a job that includes changes in salary (within the same salary bracket), status, and responsibilities, for example, an employee who moves from a secretary in marketing to a secretary in public relations. The jobs are at the same level but in different departments.

6.3.2 Promotion as an external motivator for employees

There comes a time when all employees who have been in the same position for many years perform their current duties without much thought – these activities become second nature to them. With their experience, these workers become highly productive and are able to teach others in the workplace. In this situation, the employees may feel that they have no more challenges and could become despondent.

DEFINITION

peers – employees at the same level as the employee

When employees reach this point, management should recognise that these employees need new challenges to enable them to continue their growth and development. In this case, management should be ready to promote them to higher ranks. If this is not done, these employees could move to other organisations.

There are many reasons for promoting or transferring personnel to other positions in the business. These include:

- enabling employees to keep up-to-date with changes in the organisation
- giving employees an opportunity to develop their skills and abilities
- giving temporary cover while a colleague in another department is on leave
- sharing best practice or ability in the organisation
- giving on-the-job training to new employees
- exposing employees to areas that interest them
- encouraging growth in the organisation
- giving employees exposure in areas where there are better promotion opportunities
- enabling employees to get skills and experience in key areas of the organisation.

Figure 6.5 Promotion motivates people who work hard and adds value to a business.

6.3.3 Preparing employee for a promotion

When is an employee ready for a promotion? These are some of the questions management could look at as a guide when deciding whether to promote someone in the organisation:

- Has the employee has mastered their current job roles?
- Has the employee introduced new and better ways of completing their job?
- Does the employee complete regular tasks well before the due date?
- Does the employee guide junior staff to complete certain activities?
- Does the employee look for new and different challenges within the work environment, especially by volunteering to learn new skills?
- Has the employee successfully completed a higher educational qualification?

- Does the employee receive positive comments from customers and colleagues on different tasks that were completed?
- Has the employee's 360-degree feedback from managers, peers, supervisor, subordinates, and customers been mainly positive?

Management's choice

Once management has found an employee deserving of promotion, it becomes necessary to start the process of motivating for a promotion. The manager will put a business case together with a list of the employee's major achievements, skills, abilities, experience, and qualifications. The manager would then make a recommendation for the employee to be promoted. The business case is kept on the employee's staff file and used to support an application that the employee may make when a higher position becomes available. The recommendation is added to the employee's interview pack and used by the recruiting manager when considering potential candidates to fill a vacancy.

Training and development

Effective training and development is crucial in preparing an employee for promotion. The training needs start from performance appraisals, which shows areas for development. Training programmes and developmental activities that can help an employee to grow and develop for the next job are then identified and put in place. This process continues throughout the employee's career.

> **Flashback:** Refer to Module 5, Unit 5.5, for more details on the difference between training and development.

Power break 6.3   INDIVIDUAL WORK

Read the following scenario and answer the questions that follow:

Following on from your performance evaluation in Power break 6.2, your manager has named your junior secretary as an employee who could be promoted. Your manager has asked you to help the junior secretary to prepare for promotion.

1   Write a letter of recommendation for the junior secretary to be considered for the next available position in the administration department.
2   Help the junior secretary to prepare for the application process. This includes structuring her CV. List the main sections that should be included in a CV.
3   How would your recommendation letter change if the junior secretary was to be transferred to another department?

UNIT 6.4 Disciplinary action

Not all employee work performance is excellent or above average. There are times where an employee has breached the organisation's code of conduct and may need disciplinary action to correct the behaviour.

6.4.1 Difference between grievances and disciplinary action

A grievance is an official complaint over something that is believed to be unfair or wrong that is given by an employee to management to address. Employees should feel free to raise their concerns with management, whether they are represented by a union or staff organisation or not.

Disciplinary action is taken when an employee does not adhere to the code of conduct. It is management communicating to the employees about poor work performance or unacceptable behaviour.

Disciplinary action can take on many forms, such as:
- a verbal warning
- a written warning
- a final written warning
- suspension without pay (for a limited period)
- demotion (as an alternative to dismissal)
- dismissal.

6.4.2 Handling grievances and disciplinary matters

When faced with grievances and disciplinary matters, the organisation needs to adopt different strategies to ensure that they achieve the outcome they want.

Policy

A code of conduct is the rules and regulations (policy) that an organisation puts in place to control employees' behaviour. This document lays down what type of behaviour is unacceptable and not allowed at work. It also outlines the processes and procedures that would be followed in different situations.

> **DEFINITION**
>
> **disciplinary action** – action taken when an employee does not adhere to the code of conduct; it is management communicating to the employees about poor work performance or unacceptable behaviour

Process for dealing with a grievance

Figure 6.6 outlines the process to be followed in dealing with a grievance.

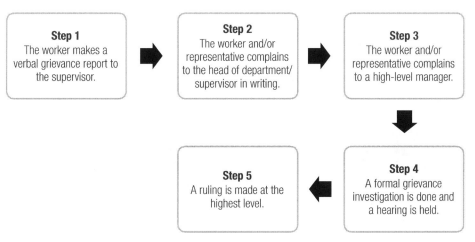

Step 1
The worker makes a verbal grievance report to the supervisor.

Step 2
The worker and/or representative complains to the head of department/supervisor in writing.

Step 3
The worker and/or representative complains to a high-level manager.

Step 5
A ruling is made at the highest level.

Step 4
A formal grievance investigation is done and a hearing is held.

Figure 6.6 Steps in the grievance procedure.

Process for dealing with disciplinary matters

For the disciplinary process to be legally recognised, the employee must:

- receive adequate notice of the hearing
- be informed of the date and time of the hearing, and the details of the charges
- be present at the hearing
- be allowed representation by either a fellow employee or union member
- be allowed to call witnesses and may question any witnesses called.

The following points are also important:

- Minutes must be kept of the hearing.
- An impartial presiding officer should hear the matter.
- The employee must be told of the final decision.
- The employee may appeal the ruling on the matter.
- The employee is considered innocent until proven guilty.

Figure 6.7 In a disciplinary hearing, the employee is considered innocent until proven guilty.

Types of offences

The disciplinary action taken for a breach of the code of conduct will depend on the severity of the offence. An offence is considered either as minor offence, a serious offence, or a very serious offence.

Minor offences include:

* arriving late for work, reporting late after lunch or tea break
* being away from work for no reason for a long time
* wasting time and deliberately working slowly.

In the case of minor offences, the employee could be offered a **consultation** to try to discuss the offence(s).

Tables 6.2 and 6.3 show the disciplinary action for serious and very serious offences.

Table 6.2 Disciplinary action for serious offences

Type of offence	First offence	Second offence	Third offence
1. Absenteeism 2. Continually late 3. Abusing sick leave 4. Inability to perform duties in time 5. Dishonesty 6. Disloyalty 7. Disregarding procedures 8. Leaving the workplace without permission 9. Clock-card offences 10. Misusing company property 11. Negligence in performance of duty 12. Poor work performance 13. Sleeping on duty 14. Violating company rules and regulations	First written warning	Final written warning	Disciplinary hearing If guilty, then dismissal
15. The possession of harmful substances	Final written warning.	Disciplinary hearing. If guilty, then dismissal	
16. Being under the influence of intoxicating substance during working hours	Send home The next day give warning and offer support.	Send home. The next day give a second warning.	Send home and dismiss after a disciplinary hearing.

DEFINITION

consultation – a meeting to give advice and make decisions to resolve problems

Table 6.3 Disciplinary action for very serious offences

Type of offence	First offence	Second offence
1. Ignoring safety rules 2. Intimidation 3. Sexual harassment 4. Refusing to obey orders 5. A threat to personal safety and property 6. Unauthorised possession of company property	Final written warning	Summary dismissal
7. Assault 8. Possession of dangerous weapons 9. Theft 10. Deliberate damage to persons or business property 11. Fraud 12. Fighting on the company premises	Summary dismissal	

The role of unions and staff organisations in grievances and disciplinary actions

As shown in the process for dealing with grievances and disciplinary matters, the employee may have a representative, usually from a union or staff organisation, present during any hearing.

Labour unions act on behalf of workers and ensure that employers do not mistreat workers or adversely affect workers economically and socially. Employees pay a monthly membership fee to the union for their support and assistance in labour or other matters. In a grievance and/or disciplinary action, the labour union serves as an **arbitrator** between the employer and the employee.

Staff organisations are like trade unions and represent employees in grievances and disciplinary actions. The difference is that staff organisations are run by volunteers.

6.4.3 Procedure when disciplinary action is taken

This section discusses the procedures that can be followed when disciplinary action is taken or when settling disputes in the workplace.

Collective bargaining agreement

A collective bargaining agreement is a legal contract for a specific period setting out the terms and conditions for an employer represented by a trade union or staff organisation. This includes the working conditions, remuneration structure, hours of work, leave conditions, and dispute-resolution processes.

> **DEFINITION**
>
> **arbitrator** – another name for the third party in a dispute-settling procedure

Mediation and arbitration

When collective bargaining has been unsuccessful, the employer and the employees can use a mediator, who tries to get the parties to agree on terms and conditions of employment. The mediator cannot legally force the parties to reach an agreement.

Arbitration is like mediation, except that the arbitrator, usually the Commission for Conciliation, Mediation and Arbitration (CCMA), can legally enforce a ruling to help the parties to come to an agreement.

6.4.4 Types of sanction

When employees do not follow the organisation's code of conduct, the organisation can sanction and act against those employees. Table 6.4 shows the types of sanction that an organisation may apply.

Table 6.4 Types of sanction

Type of sanction	Transgression	Sanction aim	Duration of sanction
Informal verbal warning	Not a serious transgression; likely a first offence	**Corrective**	The sanction is not recorded as a formal warning.
Formal verbal warning	A not-too-serious offence (likely a first offence), but one that goes against the disciplinary code	Corrective	The sanction is recorded and is valid for three months.
First written warning	Multiple, but less serious, transgression.	Corrective	The sanction is recorded and valid for six months.
Final written warning	More serious transgression or if the employee does not stop committing less serious transgressions	Corrective	The sanction is recorded and valid for six months.
Transfer	Fairly serious transgression against another employee or against the business	**Punitive**	The employee can be permanently or a temporarily moved to another job in the business.
Suspension	Serious misconduct is suspected; the transgression is so serious that the employee cannot be at work while an investigation is ongoing	Punitive	The employee is not allowed to come to work while the investigation is ongoing. The employee can also be suspended for a transgression already investigated. The suspension is without pay for a period defined by management.

continued on next page …

> **DEFINITIONS**
>
> **corrective sanction** – something that the employer does to get the employee to change their workplace behaviour
>
> **punitive sanction** – something that the employer does, when the employee behaves very badly or repeatedly commits less serious misconduct, to stop the employee from harming the business

Type of sanction	Transgression	Sanction aim	Duration of sanction
Demotion	Serious misconducted is proved	Punitive	The employee is not dismissed but given a less important job or one on a lower salary scale. This can last until the employee earns another promotion to a better job.
Dismissal	Usually applied for very serious misconduct.	Punitive	An employee's dismissal is permanent.

Power break 6.4 INDIVIDUAL WORK

Six months after appointing a new junior secretary you discover that she lied about her qualifications and is producing work of a substandard quality. You need to prepare the documents for a disciplinary action against her.

UNIT 6.5 Dismissal and retrenchment

This unit discusses the circumstances under which an employee could leave a company. These include:

- dismissal
- retrenchment
- redundancy
- lay-off
- retirement
- medical boarding
- summary dismissal.

6.5.1 Dismissal

An employee's contract of employment may be ended for disciplinary- or non-disciplinary reasons. For a **dismissal** to be considered fair it must be both **substantively** and **procedurally fair**.

> **DEFINITIONS**
>
> **dismissal** – involves ending or stopping a worker's services
>
> **substantively fair** – the employer has a valid reason before he/she can end an employee's contract of service
>
> **procedurally fair** – the employer has followed the necessary procedure before he/she dismisses an employee

6.5.2 Retrenchment

Retrenchment and redundancy occur when an employee's services are no longer needed due to no fault of the employee. Retrenchment occurs when the organisation is not growing or making a profit and is forced to cut costs to help bring the business to a healthy position.

These are guidelines for a fair retrenchment:

- Employees and trade unions must be given enough notice of the possibility of retrenchments.
- The organisation should consult with the employees and trade unions on the criteria that will be followed to decide on any possible job losses.
- Voluntary severance packages and early retirement packages should be made available to employees so that they are given an opportunity to leave on their own terms.
- All alternatives must be considered before staff are retrenched.
- If the organisation is considering selling off parts of the organisation, they should negotiate with whoever is buying that section of the business to include the existing staff in the affected section.
- People who may be retrenched should be told well in advance that their positions could be affected by the proposed retrenchment.
- The organisation should support the people to be retrenched by helping to find them alternative employment and by offering financial counselling on how best to manage any lump sum payments made on retrenchment.

6.5.3 Redundancy

Redundancy occurs when the organisation undergoes an organisational change and certain jobs are considered unnecessary or redundant.

6.5.4 Lay-off

Employers will lay-off staff as a temporary measure especially during a downturn in the economy. Once the economy has recovered sufficiently, the employer can re-hire the employees. The lay-off becomes permanent if the things do not improve.

6.5.5 Retirement

Employees retire when reaching retirement age. They could also be offered an early retirement during a retrenchment process. The employer should provide the employees

> **DEFINITIONS**
>
> **retrenchment** – the dismissal of a worker when the company does not grow or make a profit
>
> **redundancy** – occurs when the organisation undergoes an organisational change and certain jobs are considered unnecessary or redundant

with support and guidance to prepare for retirement. As mentioned in Unit 6.1, a pension is paid monthly to the retired employees. The company could also give the pensioners medical aid cover.

6.5.6 Medical boarding

Employees can request to be medically boarded based on a medical condition that affects their productive work in an organisation. The employees will have to undergo stringent medical tests by both their own doctors and the organisation's appointed doctors. A medical boarding is treated the same as an early retirement and offers the same benefits as a retirement.

6.5.7 Summary dismissal

Table 6.5 shows the things that make a normal employer/employee relationship impossible and are considered as grounds for summary dismissal.

Table 6.5 Grounds for a summary dismissal

Ground for dismissal	Explanation
Dishonesty	An employee accepts a bribe or steals money from the organisation.
Negligence	An employee does not do work to the required standard and someone else completes the work.
Incompetence	An employee cannot successfully complete an activity.
Disobedience	An employee does not to obey the rules or instructions/orders of someone in authority.
Rudeness and disrespectfulness	An employee is rude or shows lack of manners especially when dealing with customers, managers, or colleagues.
Unreasonable absence due to illness	An employee is absent from work without notifying the management and does not produce a medical certificate when needed.
Misconduct	An employee shows unacceptable or inappropriate behaviours in the workplace.
Bringing the organisation into disrepute	An employee's behaviour or conduct leads to the organisation being seen in bad light, especially by the public.
Breach of confidentiality	An employee gives out vital information (leaks the information) of the organisation to anyone outside of the organisation.

Power break 6.5 INDIVIDUAL WORK

At the end of the disciplinary process, it was decided that you need to inform your junior secretary that she will be dismissed. Describe the disciplinary process and the process of dismissal that you need to follow.

WHAT DO WE KNOW AND WHERE TO NEXT?

This module discussed direct and indirect remuneration and salary scales. We also covered performance evaluation, promotions, transfers, and disciplinary actions. The unit concluded looking at dismissals and retrenchments.

The final module discusses the important aspects of supervision and motivation.

Revisiting the learning objectives

Now that you have completed this module you should have achieved the learning objectives listed in the table below.

Learning objective	What you have learned	✔
Briefly explain the remuneration of staff.	Remuneration covers both direct remuneration (gross salary less deductions) and indirect remuneration (fringe benefits).	☐
Explain the aims and methods of performance evaluation in general and elucidate on how performance evaluation could be carried out for junior secretaries and secretaries/management assistants.	• The aim of a performance evaluation is to find the strengths, weaknesses, opportunities, and threats that an employee has. • Secretaries/management assistants and junior secretaries and can do a self-evaluation, 360-degree feedback, bell curve analysis, etc. for effective performance appraisals.	☐
Elucidate on the promotion of staff.	Based on positive feedback and strong performances in performance evaluations, certain employees can be found as potential candidates for promotion posts. The application is supported by a recommendation letter, an updated comprehensive CV and is concluded by signing a letter of appointment to the new position.	☐
Explain disciplinary action.	Disciplinary action is taken by management against employees that do not adhere to the code of conduct.	☐
Explain in detail the procedure to be followed when disciplinary action is taken against an employee.	For fair disciplinary action to occur the following should be in place. • The employee is told well in advance of the hearing, including the date, time, and venue and reasons for the action. • The employee is entitled to be represented by a union or staff organisation representative.	☐

continued on next page ...

Learning objective	What you have learned	✔
	• The employee is treated as innocent until proven guilty. • The presiding officer is impartial. • The employee may appeal any decision taken.	
Differentiate between dismissal, retrenchment, lay-off and retirement of staff.	Dismissal is when an employee's services are ended or stopped. Retrenchment occurs when the organisation is not growing or making a profit and decide to reduce the staff to make the business profitable again. Lay-off is when staff are asked to leave an organisation temporarily due to weakness in the economy, employees are rehired if the situation improves. Retirement is when staff reach retirement age and are paid a monthly pension.	☐
Explain in detail the process of dismissal of an employee, also stating the requirements according to policy, law and labour unions.	A dismissal needs to be substantively fair and procedurally fair. The organisation must have followed the right processes before dismissing an employee.	☐

Assessment

1. Multiple choice

Choose the correct answer from the various options provided. Choose only A, B, C or D and write it next to the question number.

1.1 _____ is when management and staff try to settle disputes among themselves internally.

    A   Mediation

    B   Arbitration

    C   Collective bargaining

    D   Neutral intermediate

1.2 _____ is when a third party objectively analyses all the relevant facts and then passes judgement in favour of one of the parties.

    A   Mediation

    B   Arbitration

    C   Collective bargaining

    D   Neutral intermediation

1.3 _____ is not insurance an employee receives with a pension.

    A   Medical insurance

    B   Compensation insurance

    C   Unemployment insurance

    D   Casualty insurance

1.4 Ending or terminating a worker's services following different work-related offences, such as negligence, disloyalty, theft, and misconduct, is called _____.

    A   dismissal

    B   retrenchment

    C   retirement

    D   a lay-off

1.5 Which of the following is accepted as an arbitrator in South Africa?

    A   COSATU

    B   CCMA

    C   SACP

    D   NEHAWU

                                 (5 × 1 = 5)

                                       [5]

2. True or false

Choose whether the following statements are True or False. Write down the number of the question and 'true' or 'false'.

2.1 A grievance procedure is when a worker reports any work-related problem to a manager.

2.2 Retrenchment and retirement mean an employee is forced to resign.

2.3 Employees get paid during annual leave.

2.4 Performance influences the level of productivity of the employee.

2.5 A grievance is a form of upward communication from worker to manager with regards to any work-related problem, unhappiness, or other issues.

$(5 \times 1 = 5)$

[5]

3. Match the columns

Choose a description from Column B that matches the word/item in Column A. Write only the letter (A–E) next to the question number.

Column A	Column B
3.1 Consultations	A. This is another name for the third party in a dispute-settling procedure.
3.2 Policy	B. This refers to sideways movement in a job that includes changes in salary (within the same salary bracket), status, and responsibilities.
3.3 Arbitrator	C. This involves ending or terminating a worker's services.
3.4 Transfer	D. This relates to rules and procedures that are in place, so people know what to do in certain situations.
3.5 Dismissal	E. This means giving advice and making decisions to resolve problems.

$(5 \times 2 = 10)$

[10]

4. Short questions

4.1 Distinguish between a transfer and a promotion. $(2 \times 2 = 4)$

4.2 Explain the difference between a conflict and a grievance. (4)

4.3 Outline five reasons why transfers take place in the workplace. $(5 \times 2 = 10)$

4.4 Name seven grounds for summary dismissal. (7)

4.5 Define retrenchment. (1)

[26]

5. Long questions

5.1 Each organisation has a policy for handling grievances and ultimately disciplinary action. Fill in the missing information in the disciplinary code below next to the question number (5.1.1–5.1.5).

Offence	First incidence	Second incidence	Third incidence
Theft	5.1.1		
Negligence	Written warning	5.1.2	Termination of employment
Clock card offences	Severe written warning	5.1.3	Dismissal
Fraud	5.1.4		
Drinking/drunk at work	5.1.5	Written warning	Suspension

$(5 \times 2 = 10)$

5.2 Discuss six steps in preparing an employee for a promotion with reference to training and development. (6 × 2 = 12)

5.3 Name seven sanctions that can be imposed for transgressing the disciplinary code of an organisation. (7)

[29]

6. Case study

6.1 Read through the case study and answer the questions that follow.

> **Go-go Carts**
>
> Sammy and Rudi are two employees from Go-go Carts. Sammy is the supervisor and Rudi is the administrative assistant. They normally don't get along well as Rudi will sometimes insult Sammy in front of other junior colleagues. At one point, Sammy couldn't hold his anger and ended up physically assaulting Rudi.

6.1.1 Discuss three procedures that Go-go Carts employees can follow to settle disputes. (4 × 3 = 12)

6.1.2 Advise Rudi on the best procedure to choose when resolving the dispute between him and Sammy. (2)

6.2 Read the following scenario and then answer the questions.

> Janet is a N6 management assistant student from Southfield College. There are 2 000 students enrolled in the college. Janet works part-time in the tuck shop during break times and can purchase food and cooldrinks at cost price. Occasionally Janet uses her staff discount to buy some food for her friends. The owner of the tuck shop was very angry when she realised what Janet was doing and decided to fire her.

6.2.1 Do you think Janet's conduct was professional? Motivate your answer. (3)

6.2.2 According to Janet's contract of employment, either the employer or the employee can give 24 hours' notice. What other particulars must appear in a contract of employment? (4 × 2 = 8)

[25]

Grand total: 100 marks

SUPERVISION AND MOTIVATION

This module considers the following aspects of supervision and motivation:

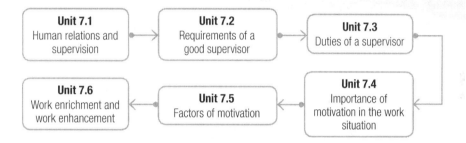

Unit 7.1
Human relations and supervision
→
Unit 7.2
Requirements of a good supervisor
→
Unit 7.3
Duties of a supervisor
→
Unit 7.4
Importance of motivation in the work situation
←
Unit 7.5
Factors of motivation
←
Unit 7.6
Work enrichment and work enhancement

Learning objectives

After completing this module, you should be able to do the following:

- Briefly explain the role of the top-level secretary/management assistant as supervisor and motivator.
- Explain in detail human relations and supervision by the secretary/management assistant.
- Explain the requirements of a good supervisor.
- Compile a guideline/office manual for the duties of a supervisor.
- Explain the importance of motivation of office workers with special reference to the motivation of different levels of staff in the secretarial division.
- Explain the factors of motivation.
- Explain examples of work enrichment and work enhancement as methods of developing and motivating secretarial staff.

Key terms

liaison	supervisor	work enrichment
superior	work enhancement	

Starting point

This last module of Office Practice N6 discusses the important aspects in the secretarial career field, namely, supervision and motivation. Verushna is excited to gain this knowledge that can help her, as a secretary/managerial assistant, to be confident of taking on the responsibility of successfully leading a secretarial team.

Figure 7.1 A supervisor meeting with her team

UNIT 7.1 Human relations and supervision

As a secretary/management assistant, you need to grow and develop in an organisation. There may even be an opportunity to be promoted to a position where one, two or a few junior staff members will report to you. To prepare for this exciting opportunity, we look at what you need to know and do in a supervisory role.

7.1.1 Role of the secretary/management assistant as supervisor and motivator

This section explores the secretary/management assistant's important roles as **supervisor** and motivator.

Role as supervisor

A supervisor is someone entrusted to check and control certain employees' performance of assigned tasks or activities. This involves hiring, firing, rewarding, disciplining, promoting and transferring of employees. Figure 7.2 shows a typical organisational structure of a department in a business, with the senior secretary responsible for the junior secretary, filing clerk and administrative support personnel in the department.

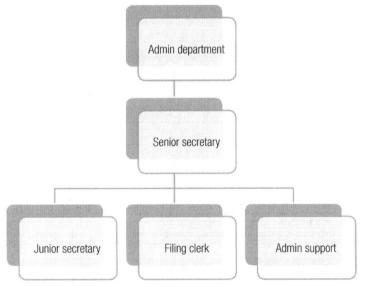

Figure 7.2 An example of an administration department's organisational structure

> **DEFINITION**
>
> **supervisor** – someone entrusted to check and control certain employees' performance of assigned tasks or activities. This involves all managerial responsibilities

Role as motivator

As a motivator, you (as a secretary/management assistant) need to ensure that the employees who report to you deliver work of a high quality within the required timeframe set for each activity. This means that the you should clearly understand what the employee needs to do and by when it should be done.

All employees have different personalities, skills and abilities and you will have to use different techniques to motivate everyone. You could use internal or external motivational techniques, such as:

- reward and recognition
- bonuses
- promotions
- praise and encouragement.

7.1.2 Human relations and supervision

You, as the supervisor, will work closely with all employees who report to you. This will involve communicating with **superiors**, subordinates and colleagues/equals. You should work on these relationships as this will ensure that you lead the team effectively.

Relationship with superiors

When dealing with superiors, you must observe correct office protocol and must either make an appointment with the superior or informally request a few minutes of the superior's time to discuss the matter(s) in hand. You should respect the time of your superior and must keep to the agenda for their meeting. During such a meeting, you could:

- discuss grievances that the employees would like to bring to management's attention
- give feedback on employees' activities
- give inputs on the employees' achievements
- request management to clear any stumbling blocks that may have been identified
- request machinery or equipment to improve the productivity of the employees
- make recommendations for potential promotions.

Relationship with subordinates

You, as supervisor, should work towards building up good relationships with employees. You should try to understand the employee's ability (what they can or cannot do) and their

> **DEFINITION**
>
> **superior** – someone who is in a senior management position

potential (whether they could still grow and develop further). To help build a relationship with a subordinate, you could:

- hold face-to-face meetings with subordinates to discuss work-related issues
- give subordinates written instructions, feedback or information using, for example, email messages, instant messages and letters
- give subordinates training manuals or procedures to refer to whenever they are uncertain about what needs to be done to complete activities.
- give subordinates regular reports on their progress on targets.

Relationship with colleagues/equals

A supervisor will have to build relationships with colleagues/equals within the organisation and will have to find ways of working with different personality types. This will help to ensure that the organisations' goals and objectives are met.

Table 7.1 shows some of the personality types that a supervisor will meet in a typical office environment.

Table 7.1 Personality types found in an office environment

Personality type	Description
The gossip	Gossips constantly talks about other people behind their backs.
The complainer	Complainers use every opportunity to complain about all things.
The flirt	Flirts are people who enjoy playing with other people's emotions and may even use this to get what they want.
The harasser	Harassers are people who sexually harasses others. As discussed in Module 3, sexual harassment or any other form of harassment has no place in the office environment.
The snob	Snobs do not get along with colleagues at lower levels of the organisation and may even be rude to staff.
The shy person	Shy people do not easily take part in any activities, especially those involving the opposite sex. It may be difficult to communicate with them.
The scatterbrain	Scatterbrains change their minds about decisions and sometimes forget what they said. They also tend to leave documents all over the office.

Power break 7.1 INDIVIDUAL TASK

What motivation technique will you use as a motivator to reward the following employees:

Employee	Motivation technique
1. Delia always goes the extra mile to complete tasks.	
2. Junaid tries to assist staff who may need help in tasks.	
3. Bongi always makes sure that the team interact positively with each other through different social events.	

UNIT 7.2 **Requirements of a good supervisor**

This unit covers some of the many skills a supervisor needs. These include general personal skills, such as being able to listen attentively, and specific skills as a manager, which include human skills, technical skills and conceptual skills. The unit concludes by discussing some supervisory styles used in the workplace.

7.2.1 General personal skills

To be successful in the workplace, supervisors should:
- become familiar with each subordinate's skills, abilities and personality
- try to build relationships with employees to gain their trust and respect
- guide employees, but allow them to set their own goals
- provide employees with a clear and simple description of the organisation's vision, mission and goals
- show the employees how their personal goals can help the organisation reach its goals
- work with the employees to create a plan with detailed steps to reach their own goals
- give the employees responsibilities to help them grow and develop for future roles that they would like to pursue within the organisation
- hold regular feedback sessions with employees to check on their progress on the agreed targets
- pinpoint any weak areas where employees may need training
- listen actively to any concerns that employees may raise and help them to find solutions
- where employees' work is not up to standard, work with them to help them to improve their understanding of the work
- communicate openly with employees and cultivate their trust and loyalty in the relationship

Figure 7.3 A supervisor will show the employees how their personal goals can help the organisation reach its goal.

- maintain a positive attitude in relationships with employees
- where needed, give constructive criticism so that the employees will see the benefit of changing their current approach
- be considerate of employees' points of view
- be an example in the workplace
- use incentives to motivate employees to improve their productivity
- be disciplined in the job and adhere to the organisation's code of ethics as employees will follow the example
- Allow the employee to make mistakes but be a coach/mentor to them so that they can learn from their mistakes
- be flexible and adapt to changes that happen within the organisation and within the employer-employee relationship
- value employees as parts of the team
- be willing to learn new skills and abilities.

7.2.2 A supervisor as a manager

Supervisors need to properly manage their subordinates to ensure that they can successfully handle the workload and are successful in completing their work activities.

To do this, supervisors should:
- practice good time management, focus on the important tasks and successfully deal with any urgent tasks as and when they arise
- be assertive and stand up for what they believe in without overriding the rights or opinions of others
- practice good leadership skills by taking a lead role in the workplace
- properly assign work to subordinates and team members
- encourage subordinates to work as a team when tackling projects or tasks
- have a sound knowledge of the various organisational policies and procedures
- properly train subordinates in the workplace to ensure that they know what is expected of them and how to accomplish their assigned tasks.

Over and above the skills mentioned here, supervisors need specific human, technical and conceptual skills to manage effectively.

Human skills

In the workplace, supervisors should:
- communicate with superiors, employees, and colleagues/equals
- motivate subordinates to complete the goals on time and accurately
- challenge subordinates to grow and develop as future leaders in the organisation
- deal tactfully with subordinates who do not perform as expected
- understand and have empathy for a subordinate's situation.

Technical skills

Supervisors should have the required technical skills to do their jobs well. To help subordinates understand their specific roles within the organisation, supervisors should:

- discuss, agree on and set targets for subordinates
- monitor subordinates' actual performance against the targets set
- identify the training needs of subordinates
- be skilled in using computers and the other office equipment.

Figure 7.4 A supervisor identifies the training needs of subordinates.

Conceptual skills

Conceptual skills refer to those skills needed to successfully handle problems in the workplace. As the supervisor you could solve problems by brainstorming or by using suggestions given by employees.

Solving problems involves:

- understanding the problem
- looking at what alternatives are available to solve the problem
- gathering information on each possibility
- deciding on a practical choice
- evaluating if the solution has given the desired results.

7.2.3 Supervisory styles

All supervisors are unique but will prefer a certain supervisory style. This way of supervising could be task- or people-centred. A supervisor could also prefer to use be a balanced supervisory style.

Task-centred supervisory style

When supervisors use a task-centred supervisory style, they spend most of their time planning, scheduling, and controlling work and results. They are more concerned in getting the job done than they are with the people doing the work.

People-centred supervisory style

Supervisors who use a people-centred supervisory style focus on motivating staff and looking after their personal challenges, problems and wellbeing. They try to ensure that their staff are always happy, regardless of their work performance.

Balanced supervisory style

Supervisors using a balanced supervisory style ensure that the work is completed on time and is of the expected standard. These supervisors also motivate their subordinates and see to their wellbeing.

Power break 7.2   INDIVIDUAL TASK

As a supervisor, what would you do in the following scenarios?

Scenario	What would you do?
1. Zarah-Skye and Hayden-Tyler are two new employees. What will you do as a supervisor to gain their trust?	
2. Mpho struggles to set goals for the year ahead. How could you assist Mpho?	
3. Zarah-Skye struggles to complete certain tasks on time. How would you find the areas that she needs training in to help her to complete tasks on time?	

UNIT 7.3 Duties of a supervisor

This unit defines a supervisor and discusses some key responsibilities and duties of a supervisor in the workplace. The unit concludes with a discussion of the managerial functions previously mentioned in Module 1.

7.3.1 Definition of a supervisor

A supervisor is someone entrusted to check and control certain employees' performance of assigned tasks or activities. This involves all managerial responsibilities. An effective supervisor should:
- complete a job analysis for any new position in the team
- delegate activities to employees
- set up and agree on performance targets for employees
- monitor actual performance against agreed targets
- give leadership and support to employees
- motivate employees to achieve their set targets
- understand the employees' aspirations to help them to reach their potential
- investigate allegations made against employees
- create opportunities for employees to grow and develop
- carry out training of new employees
- set up induction programmes for new employees in the team.

7.3.2 Duties of a supervisor

Two important aspects of the duties of a supervisor are **liaison** with management/subordinates and creating a pleasant work atmosphere.

Liaison with management and subordinates

Supervisors could use downward or upward communication to liaise with management and subordinates.

Downward communication
Downward communication (management to staff) entails:
- informing employees of outcomes from management meetings
- delegating projects/tasks given by management
- informing staff of changes to policies and procedures
- setting new organisational targets or objectives.

> **DEFINITION**
>
> **liaison** – a communication link between two different parties

Upward communication

Upward communication (staff to management) entails:

- presenting reports on behalf of employees
- communicating grievances or issues that concern employees
- motivating for the promotion of deserving employees
- discussing performance evaluations of employees and seeking management support where needed
- discussing salary-related matters on behalf of employees.

Creating a pleasant work atmosphere

In Module 2, we concluded that all staff members want to work in a pleasant work atmosphere. A supervisor can assist in creating a pleasant work atmosphere by:

- treating employees as adults and not as children
- resolving personal work issues in an assertive manner that makes all parties happy
- communicating openly and honestly without offending anyone
- considering other people's opinions and respecting their religious beliefs and cultures
- practicing good personal hygiene and avoiding unpleasant incidents
- keeping personal issues out of the work environment
- avoiding meddling in other people's personal lives
- avoiding office romances or situations that could result in personal heartache
- allowing employees to give input into decisions that impact them
- keeping to promises made.

7.3.3 Management functions

Table 7.2 details the managerial functions of a supervisor.

Table 7.2 The managerial functions of a supervisor

Managerial function	Responsibilities/tasks
Planning	As part of the planning role, a supervisor will: • set performance targets for the employees • schedule feedback sessions with employees • generate innovative ideas and ways to improve work methods • automate office tasks • set out policies, procedures, manuals, etc., that employees need to follow.
Leading	As part of the leading, a supervisor will: • set an example for the employees by showing them what should be done and how it should be done • motivate employees to do their best work • do performance evaluations for all employees • mentor/coach staff.
Organising	As part of the organising role, a supervisor will: • make sure that the right employee handles the right task/activity • ensure that there is effective communication within the team • hold team meetings to discuss group/team projects.

Managerial function	Responsibilities/tasks
Coordinating	As part of the coordinating role, a supervisor will: • delegate activities to employees • place things in the correct order to achieve the desired result.
Controlling	As part of the controlling role, a supervisor will: • make sure that a task/activity happens at the correct time and to the required standards • put action plans in place to meet deadlines • measure actual performance against targets.
Staffing	As part of the staffing role, a supervisor will: • place the right people in the right jobs to achieve the organisational goals • do job analyses for any new positions in the team • complete the required human resource documentation.

Power break 7.3 INDIVIDUAL TASK

As a supervisor, you notice that the morale in the office is down and staff have become more task-oriented than enjoying what they are doing. You were asked to draw up a plan to create a more pleasant and less stressful atmosphere in the workplace. Discuss at least three options that you can implement.

UNIT 7.4 Importance of motivation in the work situation

As previously shown, motivation helps personnel achieve their personal goals, irrespective of which level that staff member may be. Motivating secretarial staff starts from the day that the new employee starts in the organisation and it should continue until the day that person leaves the organisation. The motivational technique will differ based on the secretarial level as shown in Figure 1.13 in Module 1, which shows the different levels in the promotion route of the secretarial career.

7.4.1 Motivating at Level 1

As shown in the figure on page 15, the first level is where the typist, receptionist, and switchboard operator work. At this level, a supervisor will aim to build the confidence of the new or junior employee. Supervision at this level is more intense as the supervisor must check make sure that the employee understands what is needed in the job.

At Level 1, supervisors motivate by positive reinforcement of an employees' efforts and achievements. Supervisors must allow employees to make a few mistakes as they learn new skills and should praise employees for each new skill that they master.

Employees who have been at this level for a while may need to gain confidence from doing activities at a higher level. Senior staff members at this level may be more motivated if promoted to the next level.

7.4.2 Motivating at Level 2

Level 2 in the promotional route includes junior secretary, office assistant and Girl Friday positions. At this level, supervisors will have more trust in the employees and believe these employees know what is needed to get the job done.

Supervisors can motivate at this level by adding more responsibilities to the job to enable the staff to show their potential. This will build employees confidence even more. At this level:

- employees get greater satisfaction from receiving formal recognition in front of their peers for a job well done
- financial rewards are always a great motivator to keep employees excited about their jobs
- incentives, such as a paid vacation, and free or cheap services can also be used as a method of inspiring the employees
- the desire to move higher in the organisation will make the possibility of a promotion a further motivator for Level 2 staff members.

7.4.3 Motivating at Level 3

At Level 3 in the secretarial career, supervisors deal with experienced individuals. To motivate at this level, supervisors should carefully assess each employee's key performance drivers. Promotion to the top level will be the strongest motivator. To motivate at this level, a supervisor could also:

- increase the employees' responsibilities to prove that they are ready for promotion
- give deserving employees fringe benefits (travel awards, expense accounts, etc.) that are not available at lower levels
- give deserving employees financial rewards and incentives.

> **Power break** 7.4 **INDIVIDUAL TASK**
>
> As a supervisor, you are asked to give ideas to motivate your staff. Draw up an encouragement plan to help Level 1, 2 and 3 staff. Your plan should have two ideas for each level.

UNIT 7.5 **Factors of motivation**

This unit focuses on motivation and the factors that motivate workers/employees. We first describe the Hawthorne experiment, which aimed at understanding what influences workers' productivity. The unit then goes on to consider:

- factors that motivate workers
- needs as motivator
- Maslow's hierarchy of needs
- self-motivation
- management styles
- other issues, such as absence from work, exhaustion and burnout, and flexi-time.

7.5.1 Hawthorne experiment

Elton Mayo and Fritz Roethlisberge conducted the Hawthorne experiment in Chicago during the 1920s at the Hawthorne plant of the Western Electric Company. In the experiment, a group of workers were separated from the rest of the workers and variable changes applied to their working environment. The test subjects were interviewed during the experiment to find out what helped them be more productive.

The findings of the experiment were that productivity increased when:

- workplace lighting was improved
- the workstations were clean
- workers could build and work in teams
- workers could talk to one another and to their supervisors
- workers could have regular breaks.

The Hawthorne experiment showed that workers were more productive in a working environment where management made workers feel that they were important and treated them with dignity and respect. Even minor changes helped increase workers' productivity.

Figure 7.5 A group of office workers meeting to discuss ideas

7.5.2 Factors that motivate workers

This section covers some of the basic factors that motivate workers.

Desires

Early researchers felt that worker's motivation was driven by their desire to satisfy needs and they would do anything to meet those needs. For example, if a worker has the desire to travel to an exotic destination, that worker will work to earn extra money to be able to afford the trip.

Reward and recognition

Most workers find pleasure in receiving a reward or recognition for a job well done, especially if this recognition is given in front of their co-workers.

Praise and encouragement

When a supervisor or a manager praises or encourages workers for excellent work, these workers will try to keep up the good work to repay the faith that the supervisor or manager has shown in them.

Personality type

According to the Myers-Briggs Type Indicator, based on Carl Jung's theory of psychological types, there are four dimensions to a person's personality preferences.

1. Extravert (E) vs. Introvert (I). How we gain energy. Extraverts like company and socialising and gain energy by being with others. On the other hand, introverts gain energy from the inner world.
2. Sensing (S) vs. Intuitive (N). How we make decisions. A sensing person takes in information via their the five senses. On the other hand, an intuitive person is an abstract person and takes in information via patterns and impressions.
3. Thinking (T) vs Feeling (F). How we make decisions. Thinkers base their decisions on fact (use their heads), whereas, feelers base their decisions on values (use their hearts).
4. Judging (J) vs. Perceiving (P). Judges prefer a planned, structured world, where perceivers prefer an open-ended world. Judges like to complete a job before going on to the next one, whereas, perceivers start many things without finishing.

A combination of each of these dimensions make up to sixteen different personality types. For example: an ESFP personality is an Extrovert, Sensing, Feeling and Perceiving personality.

What motivates each personality type will govern how the supervisor can reach those employees and get them to perform at peak levels.

Job satisfaction

It is a very satisfying to achieve something special or meet a target you thought impossible to reach. A typist might thing that it is impossible to achieve a typing speed of 65 to 75 words per minute, but with constant practise and learning other techniques it could be done.

7.5.3 Needs as motivator

Needs are classified into two main categories; primary needs and secondary needs.
- Primary needs are needs that people are born with. These include the need for food, water, clothing, shelter, love, sex and security.
- Secondary needs are needs that people aspire to. These include belonging, recognition, friendship, family, power and achievement.

If a worker's primary needs are satisfied, that worker will be more motivated if offered an opportunity to satisfy their secondary needs.

7.5.4 Maslow's hierarchy of needs

Psychologist Abraham Maslow's hierarchy of needs classifies human needs into five categories (refer to Figure 4.2 in Module 4, which illustrates the theory).

Physiological needs

Physiological needs are the basic basic/primary needs that should form the base of our existence (need for breathing, food, water, housing, sleep, sex, etc).

Safety needs

Safety needs are part of the primary needs and include the need for security of employment, resources, family, health and physical protection.

Love/belonging needs

Love/belonging needs can only be satisfied once the social and other needs are satisfied.

Esteem needs

Esteem needs involve what people think of themselves (their self-concept) and what others think of them (status and respect) and includes the need for power, achievement, independence and self-confidence.

Self-actualisation needs

Self-actualisation needs refer to the need for personal development and the use of all our talents to become all that we are capable of. Examples include being promoted to management, getting a sought-after qualification or writing a book, poem or a song.

7.5.5 Self-motivation

Everyone is responsible for their own happiness. In the same way, employees are responsible for motivating themselves. This is especially true when employees have been in a specific position for a long time or are more experienced than their supervisor. Employees do not rely on their manager/supervisor for motivation but will take the initiative to set personal goals that they want to achieve. For example, if employees want to gain experience selling to customers they can talk to the salespeople in the organisation to get a better understanding of the sales process. They can also enrol in online courses to help develop other skills and abilities.

Table 7.3 shows some techniques that employees could use to motivate themselves.

Table 7.3 Self-motivation techniques

Self-motivation technique	What can you, as an employee, do?
Mentors/role models	Select someone you can look up to. Find out what has made that person a success and do the same.
Motivational speakers	Listen to motivational speakers to help you find a positive approach to life and work challenges.
Education	Enrol for a higher qualification or do a course that can help you grow and develop.
Readers and leaders	Read often – the more you read, the more you will be exposed to other ideas, visions, other ways of thinking, etc.
Online courses	Enrol for an online course. With the advances in the internet, more training material has become available for people to do self-study on a wide range of topics. This will improve your skills.
Develop a personal mission statement	Put into words what you want to achieve in the short, medium, and long term.
Create a collage of your ideal life	Create a visual representation of what you want to achieve. This will help you stay focused, especially when you feel like giving up.
Track progress	Once you have set your personal goals, track your progress to see if you need to change anything.
Keep up-to-date with changes in technology	Learn to use the latest technology. This will give you an advantage in the job market.
Talk to experts	Talk to experts. This will help you gain more insight into the specific field that you are interested in.
Volunteer for projects	Volunteer for certain tasks. This will give you experience in those projects.
Follow through on plans	Make plans to achieve goals. More importantly, follow through on those plans and do what is needed to achieve the goals.
Keep moving forward	Once you have started something, it is important to keep moving forward.

7.5.6 Management styles

When considering a management style to adopt, a manager should consider the task, the people, and the situation that needs to be managed. Here are some examples of different management styles that can be used.

Participating management

When adopting a participating management approach, a manager works with the employees to make decisions (they take part in the process). The employees give input into the goals that they need to achieve. The manager motivates by rewarding team effort.

Management by objectives

When adopting a management by objectives approach, management sets objectives for all the employees in the organisation. These objectives are linked to the overall organisational objective. The organisational goals are passed down to employees, who give very little input.

Quality circles

When adopting a quality circles approach, employees work in groups to define and solve quality- or performance-related problems. Employees help each other to meet their targets. This approach is mainly used in projects.

Consultation

When adopting a consultation approach, a manager takes on the role of a consultant to the employees. The approach is aimed at the long-term personal development of employees. The employees are in full control of setting their own goals and the manager only consults on how best to achieve the set goals. Employees are motivated by being given opportunities for personal development.

> **Did you know?** There are more management styles that are used.
> - Directive: These managers seek immediate compliance from the employees: 'Do it the way I tell you'.
> - Authoritative: These managers give long-term direction and vision to employees.
> - Pacesetting: These managers requires work of a high standard of excellence and will do the tasks themselves to ensure that they meet the standard.

7.5.7 Absence from work

An organisation should have a policy in place to limit an employee's absence from the work. It should specify how long an employee may be absent and when a doctor's letter is needed. The normal leave cycle is as follows:
- sick leave – 36 days over a three-year cycle
- family responsibility leave – three days
- study leave – 20 days over a three-year cycle
- maternity leave – four months
- paternity leave – three days.

However, in all professions, including the secretarial field, there will be times where the supervisor needs to deal with unexpected absenteeism from work. The supervisor will have to arrange temporary cover for the absent employee, especially if the absence is for a lengthy period. When an employee is absent from work, the supervisor must first try to find out the reason for this absence. The absence may be due to unforeseen circumstances or other underlying reasons.

These are some possible reasons for absence from work:

- The employee may be physically unwell (cold, flu, stomach bug, etc.).
- The employee may have been to a hospital for treatment or a check-up or could have been admitted to hospital for some reason.
- The employee could have been in an accident or has suffered an injury.
- The employee may be overworked.
- The employee may be having difficulty getting along with colleagues.
- The employee may be suffering from stress due to personal or work-related issues.
- The employee may have family responsibilities (a sick loved one or death in the family).
- The employee may have personal issues to attend to (marital problems or other relationship problems).
- The employee may be on maternity or paternity leave
- The employee may be studying for or writing an exam.
- The employee may have problems with public transport due to strikes or problems with the infrastructure.
- The employee may have experienced violence or unrest in an area affecting the transport to work.
- The employee's transport may have broken down.
- The employee may lack finances to get to work.
- An employee may have legal issues (attending a court case or seeing a lawyer for some reason).
- An employee may be taking part in a political demonstration.
- An employee may have problems with drugs and/or alcohol.

To help reduce regular absenteeism, an organisation can adopt a 'no-work-no-pay' policy. An organisation could also lay down that an employee may not be absent from work within eight weeks of being absent previously. If the employee is absent within the eight weeks period, then the employee must produce a valid doctor's certificate to support the reason for absence. The organisation could also insist that an employee should undergo a medical examination before being appointed. This will give the recruiting manager an assessment of the employee's health.

When an employee is absent from work, the supervisor should review the reasons for the absence and try to solve any problems leading to the absence.

To help reduce absenteeism, a supervisor could:

- keep a check on how much leave is due to the employees, and when it is due (if an employee is not taking leave it could lead to unplanned absence later)
- ask whether the organisation could help with any issues that the employee has had to deal with, for example, if the employee has chronic back pain, the organisation could perhaps arrange an ergonomic chair that gives better back support

- check the worker's productivity and quality of work as this could be an early indicator that the employee needs to rest
- encourage the employee to do exercise to help reduce stress levels
- take a walk with the employee just to chat and to get his or her mind off work, even if it only for a few minutes
- use **work enrichment** and **work enhancement** techniques to help motivate employees to get better job satisfaction and increase their desire to be at work
- use other motivation techniques to reward employees for good attendance.

> **Did you know?** Some organisations have introduced annual health checks for their employees to help the employees assess their wellness, and take pro-active measures to prevent future problems.

7.5.8 Exhaustion and burnout

Exhaustion and burnout can also lead to absenteeism from work. Exhaustion is a state when an employee has been working too long and has no energy left to continue working. Burnout refers to a state where an employee is physically, emotionally, and psychologically exhausted due to prolonged working periods in a stressful environment without proper rest periods. Burnout can be dangerous as the employee could suffer physical or psychological consequences. Symptoms of work burnout include:

- physical symptoms, such as continual tiredness, a high blood pressure, excessive weight gain or loss, excessively red eyes from lack of sleep, and nervousness
- psychological symptoms, such as moodiness, anger, depression, irritability, aggressiveness, tenseness and violence.
- behavioural symptoms, such as over- or undereating and increased use of alcohol and/or drugs.

Figure 7.6 Exhaustion is a state when an employee has been working too long and has no energy left to continue working.

> **DEFINITIONS**
>
> **work enrichment** – the process of expanding a position horizontally by adding duties
> **work enhancement** – the process of improving the quality of an employee's work

7.5.9 Flexi-time

A flexi-time policy allows employees to have some freedom in their workday. This policy lays down that employees can start or leave work at any time if they work their right number of hours for the day, week or month.

Table 7.4 gives some advantages and disadvantages of flexi-time.

Table 7.4 Advantages and disadvantages of flexi-time

Advantages of flexi-time	Disadvantages of flexi-time
There is less absenteeism as employees can attend to personal issues and still be present at work that day.	The supervisor needs to check the hours that employees have worked to make sure that they meet their working hours commitment to the organisation.
Coming to work late or leaving early are no longer issues.	Employees need security access to the office for extended periods.
Better customer support is possible as the workday can be extended by employees working flexi-time.	The system relies on trusting the employees that they will work during the late hours when other employees have left the office.
There will be reduced staff turnover as employees have more flexibility and freedom.	Public transport may not be available at the times when the employees want to start or end their workdays.
Employees can avoid the morning and evening traffic problems by starting work later and ending later.	It can be difficult to schedule meetings as all the attendees may not be available at the same time.
The organisation can sell to international customers as there will be someone available during the international customer's workday. For example: selling to customers in New Zealand needs someone to be available from midnight to 08:00.	Electricity costs are higher as the workday starts earlier and ends later.

Power break 7.5 **PAIR WORK**

In pairs, discuss whether the Hawthorne experiment or Maslow's hierarchy of needs would be most effective in motivating staff. List five reasons why it is better than the other theory.

UNIT 7.6 **Work enrichment and work enhancement**

This final unit discusses work enrichment and work enhancement. These are two important and effective motivational tools to help employees, especially senior staff members, increase their productivity and get greater job satisfaction.

7.6.1 Work enrichment

Work enrichment involves adding more tasks or activities to an existing job. It is a motivational technique used for employees that have been in a position for several years and have proven successful in managing their current workload. To practice work enrichment, a manager could:

- give accountability to employees by allowing them to take the credit or get the blame for what happens in their job
- give employees additional work to do over and above their normal work
- increase the work tempo by challenging employees to deliver regular work much earlier than when they started in the position
- control the use/overuse of resources by encouraging employees to use all available resources to get their jobs done
- enhance employees' personal growth and development by ensuring that they have the skills, abilities, and capacity to do the additional work given to them.

7.6.2 Work enhancement

Work enhancement has to do with improving the quality of employees' work. Once employees have mastered their tasks, the number of errors that occur in the workplace will reduce. To practice work enhancement, a manager could:

- reduce monotony in the workplace, which will help employees find new excitement in doing their daily tasks
- encourage employees to suggest ways of automating tasks in the office environment
- encourage employees to recommend improvements to existing work procedures
- allow certain employees to train others on existing workplace procedures.

Power break 7.6   INDIVIDUAL WORK

The table shows six scenarios. Decide whether they represent work enrichment or a work enhancement.

Activity	Work enrichment/ enhancement
1. David is asked to finish his reports two days earlier than usual.	
2. Chanel must prepare travel itineraries for four foreign visitors coming to a sales conference in June.	
3. Janine, the typist, needs to find supporting documents for a legal case that the organisation is preparing.	
4. Kosie must add a management summary to his sales forecast report.	
5. Sharon is asked to join the project team for two weeks to help with the administration backlogs.	
6. Dolan must be an understudy to Beverley, the senior secretary, before she goes on maternity leave.	

WHAT DO WE KNOW AND WHERE TO NEXT?

This module covered human relations and supervision. We first examined the requirements and duties of a good supervisor. Next, we discussed the importance of motivation in the work situation and the factors affecting motivation. The module concluded by discussing work enrichment and work enhancement.

Revisiting the learning objectives

Now that you have completed this module you should have achieved the learning objectives listed in the table below.

Learning objective	What you have learned	✔
Briefly explain the role of the top-level secretary/management assistant as supervisor and motivator.	As a supervisor, the secretary/management assistant will be responsible for the work performance of certain junior staff members/subordinates in the organisation. This includes hiring, firing, performance reviews and target setting. As a motivator, the secretary/management assistant needs to understand each employee and work out the best way to motivate that employee.	☐
Explain in detail human relations and supervision by the secretary/management assistant.	As a supervisor, the secretary/management assistant will: • deal with employee issues and provide feedback on their work performance • deal with sub-ordinates/employees about instructions given by management, work performance, target setting and feedback on issues raised, etc. The secretary/management assistant will also deal with colleagues/equals/peers and will need to know the different personality types and how to deal with each accordingly.	☐
Explain the requirements of a good supervisor.	A good supervisor should be able to: • become familiar with each subordinate's skills, abilities, and personality • build a relationship with each employee to gain their trust and respect • assist employees to set performance targets and put in place an effective plan to achieve each target • have regular feedback sessions to track employees' progress against targets.	☐
Compile a guideline/office manual for the duties of a supervisor.	A supervisor is responsible to check and control certain employees' performance and assigned tasks or activities. This will involve: • completing job analysis for new positions in the team • delegating activities to employees • setting and agreeing performance targets for employees • monitoring actual performance against the agreed targets.	☐

continued on next page …

Learning objective	What you have learned	✔
	Other aspects of the supervisor's duties include: • liaison with management and subordinates • creating a pleasant work atmosphere • management functions (planning, organising, activating/coordinating, controlling and staffing).	
Explain the importance of motivation of office workers with special reference to the motivation of different levels of staff in the secretarial division.	The supervisor must adopt different motivational strategies for employees on different levels in their secretarial careers.	☐
Explain the factors of motivation.	There are various factors of motivation including: • desires • reward and recognition • praise and encouragement • personality types • job satisfaction • needs as a motivator. The supervisor will adopt different management styles to motivate staff. These include: • participating management • management by objectives • quality circles • consultations. The supervisor will also have to deal with absence, exhaustion, flexi-time, work enrichment and work enhancement.	☐
Explain examples of work enrichment and work enhancement as methods of developing and motivating secretarial staff.	Work enrichment is about adding to the employee's job. Work enhancement is about the employee delivering higher quality work.	☐

Assessment

1. Multiple choice

Choose the correct answer from the various options provided. Choose only A, B, C or D and write it next to the question number.

1.1 Deciding employment policies is one of the duties of _____.

  A top management

  B employees

  C operating management

  D middle management

1.2 _____ is the process whereby a position is expanded horizontally by adding duties.

  A Job enlargement

  B Task enrichment

  C Job description

  D Job analysis

1.3 Emotional exhaustion, decline in personal performance, avoidance of social contact, and low productivity could result in _____.

  A absence from work

  B unhappiness

  C punishment

  D burnout

1.4 _____ is not how task enrichment takes place?

  A Accountability

  B Performance

  C Work tempo

  D Additional responsibilities

1.5 _____ is when a worker for some reason fails to arrive at the workplace.

  A Exhaustion

  B Burnout

  C Absence from work

  D Flexi-time

$(5 \times 1 = 5)$

[5]

2. True or false

Choose whether the following statements are true or false. Write down the number of the question and 'true' or 'false'.

2.1 A management style should be inconsistent all the time.

2.2 The decision-making process includes proper preparation and research.

2.3 A reward of punishment is also known as an external motivator.

2.4 Punishment is known as the external motivator and motivates a person for his hard work by means of a salary increase.

2.5 Quality circles are a participatory management technique that enlists the help of employees to help solve problems related to their own jobs.

(5 × 1 = 5)

[5]

3. Match the columns

Choose a description from Column B that matches the word/item in Column A. Write only the letter (A–E) next to the question number.

Column A	Column B
3.1 People-oriented	A. This is an approach in which the leader focuses on the tasks that need to be performed to meet certain goals.
3.2 A manager	B. This entails setting and achieving of objectives and the successful execution of duties and responsibilities to ensure a smooth flow of activities within the organisation.
3.3 Work without pay	C. This is one of the symptoms of burnout.
3.4 Task-oriented	D. This is the person who undertakes the responsibility of managing the enterprise.
3.5 Feeling of failure	E. This is a method commonly used to discourage workers from being absent from work.

(5 × 2 = 10)

[10]

4. Short questions

4.1 Give a short description of the following terms:

    4.1.1 management

    4.1.2 manager

    4.1.3 managerial success

    4.1.4 burnout   (4 × 3 = 12)

4.2 Name and explain the two basic groups of needs that motivate employees.   (2 × 2 = 4)

4.3 Name two advantages of flexi-time in the workplace.   (2 × 2 = 4)

[20]

5. Long questions

5.1 Discuss eight requirements of a supervisor as a manager.   (8 × 2 = 16)

5.2 Discuss the following skills of a good supervisor:

    5.2.1 human/interpersonal skills   (12)

    5.2.2 technical skills   (6)

    5.2.3 conceptual/thinking skills   (8)

5.3 Explain how a manager can use work enrichment and work enhancement to motivate staff.   (8)

[50]

6. Case study

Read through the case study and answer the questions that follow.

> **ROWAN & SONS**
>
> Portia has been appointed as the new senior secretary for the law firm, Rowan & Sons. Natasha, who has been a junior secretary for five years, and Amelia, who has been an admin assistant for six years, both report to Portia.
>
> In preparing for her first staff meeting with Natasha and Amelia, Portia was given their attendance information for the last three months. Natasha has been absent at least two to three days every month and only has one sick day left for her three-year cycle available. Amelia, on the other hand, has built up 30 days of her annual leave as she has not taken any leave in the last 15 months.

6.1 Given that Natasha has almost used all her sick leave, discuss five reasons for absenteeism in the workplace, and give Portia suggestions on how she can reduce Natasha's chronic absence from the office. $(10 \times 2 = 20)$

6.2 In your opinion, what risk does Amelia face? (2)

6.3 Discuss four ailments that Amelia could suffer from if she does not take leave soon. $(4 \times 2 = 8)$

[30]

Grand total: 120 marks

BIBLIOGRAPHY

Brits, S. & Coetzee, Z. (2016). *Succeed in personnel management N4 student book*. Cape Town: Oxford University Press Southern Africa (Pty) Ltd.

Cardinal, R. (2013). 6 Management styles and when best to use them - the leaders tool kit. [Online] Available at https://leadersinheels.com/career/6-management-styles-and-when-best-to-use-them-the-leaders-tool-kit/ (Accessed 3 April 2018).

CCMA (Commission for Conciliation, Mediation and Arbitration). (2018). Individual employee, employer. [Online] Available at https://www.ccma.org.za/Services/Individual-Employee-Employer/Disciplinary-procedures (Accessed 15 April 2018).

CIPC (Companies & Intellectual Property Commisssion). (2018). Maintain your company. (2018, 04 02). [Online] Available at http://www.cipc.co.za/index.php/manage-your-business/manage-your-company/ (Accessed 2 April 2018).

Computer Hope. (2017). Communication device. [Online] Available at https://www.computerhope.com/jargon/c/communication-devices.htm (Accessed 30 June 2018).

Dachis, A. (2011). How to design and create a clean organized desktop. [Online] Available at https://lifehacker.com/5864785/how-to-design-and-create-a-clean-organized-desktop (Accessed 30 June 2018).

Digital Software Development. (n.d.). Email protocols: IMAP, POP3, SMTP and HTTP. [Online] Available at http://www.emailaddressmanager.com/tips/protocol.html. (Accessed 5 March 2018).

DOL (Department of Labour, South Africa). (2017). *Employment equity act and amendments, Act summary* [Online] Available at http://www.labour.gov.za/DOL/legislation/acts/employment-equity/employment-equity-act-and-amendments (Accessed 8 April 2018).

Dworzanowski-Venter, B. (2015). *Succeed in labour relations N6 student book*. Cape Town: Oxford University Press Southern Africa (Pty) Ltd.

Evans, K. (n.d.). The advantages of using an electronic diary. [Online] Available at https://itstillworks.com/advantages-using-electronic-diary-5902998.html (Accessed 30 June 2018).

Geen, T. & Geen, D. (2017). *Succeed in office practice N5 student book*. Cape Town: Oxford University Press Southern Africa (Pty).

Geen, T. & Geen, D. (2016). *Succeed in office practice N4 student book*. Cape Town: Oxford University Press Southern Africa (Pty).

Graham, M. & Iyer, S. (2017). *Succeed in business and entrepreneurship N5 student book*. Cape Town: Oxford University Press Southern Africa (Pty).

HR Works. (2012). Recruitment policy [Online] Available at https://www.hrworks.co.za/policies/298-recruitment_policy (Accessed 8 April 2018).

Job-Interview-Site.com (n.d.). The qualities of a good supervisor. [Online] Available at: http://www.job-interview-site.com/what-makes-a-good-supervisor.htm (Accessed 19 April 2018).

Leonard, K. (2018). Advantages and disadvantages of a paperless office. [Online] Available at http://smallbusiness.chron.com/advantages-amp-disadvantages-paperless-office-40653.html (Accessed 28 June 2018).

Lumens.com. (2018). What is a lumen? What's the difference between it and a watt? [Online] Available at https://www.lumens.com/how-tos-and-advice/what-are-lumens.html (Accessed 3 May 2018).

Mack, S. (n.d.). Positive & negative effects of office automation on human resources. [Online] Available at https://yourbusiness.azcentral.com/positive-negative-effects-office-automation-human-resources-16604.html (Accessed 20 May 2018).

MacKenzie, B. (n.d.). What is a pyschological contract? [Online] Available at https://www.alchemyformanagers.co.uk/topics/6ixdhhPwDvZFjsZc.html (Accessed 8 April 2018).

Mans, A. (2016). *Succeed in personnel training N5 student book*. Cape Town: Oxford University Press Southern Africa (Pty) Ltd.

Moore, S. (2008). *Office administration, Volume 1 – Facilitation practicum*. Cape Town: CLS Publishers.

Naspers. (2018). Naspers company profile. [Online] Available at http://www.naspers.com/about (Accessed 30 May 2018).

OPP. (2018). *Myers-Briggs personality types*. [Online] Available at https://www.opp.com/en/tools/MBTI/MBTI-personality-Types (Accessed 1 June 2018).

Personal-Assistant-Tips. (n.d.). Personal-assistant-tips [Online] Available at http://www.personal-assistant-tips.com/Personal_Assistant.htm (Accessed 29 December 2017).

Rawat, S. (2014). Benefits of teamwork [Online] Available at https://www.linkedin.com/pulse/20140828060629-182026999-benefits-of-teamwork (Accessed 1 July 2018).

Reuters Staff. (2009). Timeline: Key dates in the history of the personal computer. [Online] Available at https://www.reuters.com/article/us-laptop-sb/timeline-key-dates-in-the-history-of-the-personal-computer-idUSTRE50601V20090107 (Accessed 1 July 2018).

Rheeder, L. &. Hauptfleisch. (2016). *Succeed in communication N4 student book*. Cape Town: Oxford University Press Southern Africa (Pty) Ltd.

Root, G. (2018). *Methods of performance evaluation*. [Online] Available at http://smallbusiness.chron.com/methods-performance-evaluation-1869.html (Accessed 1 July 2018).

Smart Fog. (2016). Industrial humidifier helps control static electricity in the workplace. [Online] Available at http://www.smartfog.com/industrial-humidifier-helps-control-static-electricity-workplace.html (Accessed 15 June 2018).

Smit, R. (2016). *Succeed in sales management N6 student book*. Cape Town: Oxford University Press Southern Africa (Pty) Ltd.

Stacey, E. (2007). The importance of a good CV. [Online] Available at https://www.legalsecretaryjournal.com/the_importance_of_a_good_cv (Accessed 2 July 2018).

Stats SA (Statistics South Africa). (2013). Survey of employers and the self-employed 2013. [Online] Available at http://www.statssa.gov.za/publications/P0276/P02762013.pdf (Accessed 28 May 2018).

Swanepoel, D. (1992). Ekonomie 2000 Standerd 8 1992-sillabus. Cape Town: Nasionale Opvoedkundige Uitgewery Beperk.

The DoJ&CD (Department of Justice and Constitutional Development, South Africa). (1996). The constitution of the Republic of South Africa, 1996. [Online] Available at http://www.justice.gov.za/legislation/constitution/SAConstitution-web-eng.pdf (Accessed 1 July 2018).

The Wheel. (n.d.). Shared electronic diaries. [Online] Available at http://www.wheel.ie/content/shared-electronic-diaries (Accessed 3 April 2018).

UMass Dartmouth. (n.d.). 7 Steps to effective decision making. [Online] Available at https://www.umassd.edu/media/umassdartmouth/fycm/decision_making_process.pdf (Accessed 1 July 2018).

United Nations. (n.d.). *Universal declaration of human rights*. [Online] Available at 04 05). Retrieved from http://www.un.org/en/universal-declaration-human-rights/ (Accessed 5 April 2018).

University of Minnesota. (n.d.). Need-based theories of motivation. [Online] Available at http://open.lib.umn.edu/principles management/chapter/14-3-need-based-theories-of-motivation/ (Accessed 22 April 2018).

Van der Bijl, A. (2016). *Succeed in marketing management N4 student book*. Cape Town: Oxford University Press Southern Africa (Pty) Ltd.

Van der Bijl, A. (2017). *Succeed in marketing management N5 student book*. Cape Town: Oxford University Press Southern Africa (Pty) Ltd.

Ward, S. (2017). Target marketing: Target marketing can be the key to increasing sales. [Online] Available at https://www.thebalance.com/target-marketing-2948355 (Accessed 1 July 2018).

Wasserman, H. (2012). How to start a stokvel. [Online] Available at https://www.w24.co.za/Work/Money/Starting-a-stokvel-20090907 (Accessed 2 July 2018).

Western Cape Government. (2016). How to deal with sexual harassment in the workplace. [Online] Available at https://www.westerncape.gov.za/general-publication/how-deal-sexual-harassment-workplace (Accessed 18 March 2018).

ACKNOWLEDGEMENTS

Images
Page 2 Shutterstock/India Picture; **page 7** Shutterstock/Dragon Images; **page 9** Shutterstock/Maslowski Marcin; **page 11** Pixabay/geralt; **page 12** PEP Stores; **page 13** (left) Folio/Rui Ricardo; **page 13** (middle) Shutterstock/Nerthuz; **page 13** (right) Shutterstock/Sorbis; **page 14** Shutterstock Business Images; **page 16** Shutterstock/Elena Elisseeva; **page 19** Antonio Guillem; **page 21** Shutterstock/Rawpixel.com; **page 28** Shutterstock/wavebreakmedia; **page 29** Shutterstock/Stokkete; **page 31** (top) Shutterstock/Aaron Amat; **page 31** (bottom) Pixabay/FirmBee; **page 33** Shutterstock/vectorfusionart; **page 37** (top) Shutterstock/Lemurik; **page 37** (bottom) Shutterstock/Corepics VOF; **page 39** Shutterstock/nd3000; **page 40** Shutterstock/David Hughes; **page 42** Pixabay/FirmBee; **page 44** Shutterstock/Tarzhanova; **page 46** Shutterstock/pryzmat; **page 49** Shutterstock/Myimagine; **page 52** Shutterstock/Rawpixel.com; **page 62** Shutterstock/michaeljung; **page 63** Shutterstock/Photographee.eu; **page 64** Shutterstock/Fure; **page 65** Shutterstock/fitzcrittle; **page 66** Shutterstock/encictat; **page 68** Shutterstock/Pressmaster; **page 69** Shutterstock/Rawpixel.com; **Page 70** Shutterstock/KreativKolors; **page 72** Gareth Boden; **page 73** Pixabay/geralt; **page 75** Shutterstock Olivier Le Moal; **page 78** Shutterstock/Dragon Images; **page 82** Shutterstock/wavebreakmedia; **page 86** Shutterstock/Mark; **page 97** Pixabay/rawpixel; **page 107** Marcio Shutterstock/Jose Bastos Silva; **page 111** Pixabay/rawpixel; **page 112** Shutterstock/Odua Images; **page 114** Shutterstock/Robyn Mackenzie; **page 115** Shutterstock/BEST-BACKGROUNDS; **page 118** Matej Shutterstock/Kastelic; **page 120** Shutterstock/Neil Mitchell; **page 126** Shutterstock/MinDoF; **page 129** 123RF; **page 133** OpenClipart-Vectors; **page 135** Shutterstock/Sinseehok; **page 137** Gareth Boden; **page 139** Shutterstock/Brian A Jackson; **page 142** Pixabay/rawpixel; **page 143** Shutterstock/Andrey_Popov; **page 145** Shutterstock/wavebreakmedia; **page 147** Shutterstock/Jakkarin chuenaka; **page 149** Pixabay/godoycordoba; **page 151** Shutterstock/StockLite; **page 155** Harald_Landsrath; **page 167** Shutterstock/Rasstock; **page 170** Shutterstock/ImageFlow; **page 172** 123rf/Yuriy Kirsanov; **page 174** Pixabay/mohamed_hassan; **page 177** Pixabay/ArtsyBee; **page 190** Shutterstock/BlueSkyImage; **page 194** Pixabay/geralt; **page 202** Shutterstock/Rawpixel.com; **page 208** Shutterstock/Rawpixel.com

GLOSSARY

accountability to take ownership of a task or activity whether it is completed successfully or unsuccessfully

acronym a word formed from the initial letters or groups of letters of words in a set phrase or series of words and pronounced as a separate word, such as OPEC for Organization of Petroleum Exporting Countries, or NATO for North Atlantic Treaty Organization

affirmative action the policy of giving jobs and other opportunities to members of groups, such as racial minorities or women, who might not otherwise have them

arbitrator another name for the third party in a dispute-settling procedure

automation (office) introducing computerised steps to replace a manual process

best practice the most effective and practical method or technique to achieve an objective while making the optimum use of the enterprise's resources

binary made up of two digits

breach to break a law or rule

cloud storage online space that you use to store your data, photos, music, and videos for access from any of your devices

confidentiality the entrusted way to hold important information secretly

consultation a meeting to give advice and make decisions to resolve problems

contrast compare two people or things to show the differences between them

corporate identity a lasting representation of how a firm views itself

corrective sanction something that the employer does to get the employee to change their workplace behaviour

creditor someone that the business owes money to

data link a telecommunications link that can send or receive data

disciplinary action action taken when an employee does not adhere to the code of conduct; it is management communicating to the employees about poor work performance or unacceptable behaviour

dismissal involves ending or stopping a worker's services

etiquette the correct conduct in a company/business, organisation or practice to render service and increase productivity

flash drive a small piece of equipment used to store and transfer information for computers using a USB

gatekeeper a person who controls access to a business

grievance an unfair or unjust action that may cause a person or group to lay a complaint against another person or group

harassment aggressive pressure or intimidation

hard disk drive (HDD) a computer hardware device that permanently stores and retrieves data on a computer

hardware the physical components of a computer

hierarchy the levels of authority in the organisation where the higher the position the greater the authority

horizontal organisational structure flatter organisation structure where information and orders are from the senior to all employees reporting to him/her

human resource department the company department responsible for finding, screening, recruiting, and training job applicants, as well as administering employee-benefit programmes

human resources the people who make up the workforce of an organisation, business sector, or economy

incumbent the person now in a position

indigent needy person

induction programme the process used within many businesses to welcome new employees to the company and prepare them for their new role

interview a two-way communication between an interviewer and an applicant about a position at an organisation

job analysis the process of gathering and analysing information about the content and the human requirements of jobs, as well as, the context in which jobs are performed

letterhead the heading at the top of a sheet of paper; usually consists of the name and address of the business, logo or corporate design and sometimes a background image (watermark)

liaison a communication link between two different parties

management the people that collectively manage the running of a business enterprise

market a place where buyers and sellers meet to trade goods and/or services in exchange for money

mentor a person who gives a younger or less experienced person help and advice over a period, especially at work or school

merge to join data from direct sources

monopoly when the main supplier that has the greater market share and can manipulate the market when they want to

need the desire or craving for something (goods or services) that gives us physical, social or psychological satisfaction

network server a computer system, which is used as the central repository of data and various programs that are shared by users in a network

objective (verb) not influenced by personal feelings or opinions in considering and representing facts

optical disk an electronic data storage medium that can be written to and read using a low-powered laser beam

optimal the level at which a person performs at their best or most effectively

peers employees at the same level as the employee

perception a way of regarding, understanding or interpreting something

performance evaluation the process of reviewing the work performance of an employee against the targets that were set for the employee

person includes people and other legal persona (companies or close corporations)

policy a course or principle of action adopted or proposed by an organisation or individual

probationary a time for both the employee and the organisation to assess whether the employee can do the work needed; usually a three-month period

procedurally fair the employer has followed the necessary procedure before he/she dismisses an employee

product life cycle the product life cycle has four very clearly defined stages, each with its own characteristics

proofread to find and correct mistakes in text before it is printed or put online

protocol a set of procedures that apply when communicating

psychometric test used to assess whether someone has the right aptitude, attitude, behaviour, intelligence, and other qualities needed to do a job

punitive sanction something that the employer does, when the employee behaves very badly or repeatedly commits less serious misconduct, to stop the employee from harming the business

random-access memory (RAM) the physical hardware inside a computer that temporarily stores data, serving as the computer's 'working' memory.

read-only memory (ROM) the memory from which we can only read but cannot write on it; the information is stored permanently in such memories during manufacture

recruitment the process of finding and hiring the best-qualified candidate to fill a position in the organisation

redundancy occurs when the organisation undergoes an organisational change and certain jobs are considered unnecessary or redundant

remuneration payment for work done

retrenchment the dismissal of a worker when the company does not grow or make a profit

rules of engagement written guidelines by which all team members are expected to behave, communicate, engage, support, treat, and coordinate with one another

salutation greeting normally used in written communication, for example, Dear Jane

SD card an ultra-small flash memory card designed to provide high-capacity memory in a small size; used in many small portable devices

software the programs used by a computer

spreadsheet a document in which data is arranged across rows and columns allowing the data to be calculated and/or analysed

staffing the selection and training of individuals for specific job functions and making them responsible to perform those job functions

subordinate a person under the authority or control of another within an organisation

substantively fair the employer has a valid reason before he/she can end an employee's contract of service

superior someone who is in a senior management position

supervisor someone entrusted to check and control certain employees' performance of assigned tasks or activities; involves all managerial responsibilities

synergy the combined power of a group of things when they are working together that is greater than the total power achieved by each working separately

tacit unwritten or implied without it being written

tactful dealing sensitively with others or with difficult issues

vertical organisational structure information and orders are passed from top management down to lower management

VIP Very Important Person

weightings applying different levels of importance to something

work enhancement the process of improving the quality of an employee's work

work enrichment the process of expanding a position horizontally by adding duties

written offer this offer includes the salary, pension/provident fund, medical aid, leave and other benefits that the employee will receive

INDEX

Maslow's hierarchy of needs 98, 152, 201, 204–205

media
    information *see* storing and indexing of media information
    necessity of 85
    methods of 86
    scanning of 85–87
mediation and arbitration 180 *see also* disciplinary action
medical boarding 183
memory card 47
mentor 151, 154, 195
microcomputer technology
    applications in business 34–35
    applications in wider community 36
    customer benefits 35
    impact on office workers 35
middle management 3
mission 12
motivating factors in the workplace
    desires 202
    job satisfaction 203
    needs 203
    personality type 203
    praise and encouragement 203
    reward and recognition 202
motivation
    in work situations 200–203
    Hawthorne experiment 202

N

needs as motivator 203
network server 45

O

observation method of performance evaluation 172
office automation
    communication links 38
    implications *see* implications of office automation
    influence on work environment 36–41
    principles of 29–30
    effects of changes in technology on 31–33
    effects on secretaries 30

effects on workplace layout and work routine 39–41 see also desktop arrangements; office layout; work routine
    lighting 38
    provision and maintenance of equipment and furniture 38
    temperature control 38
office
    entertaining *see* entertaining in the office
    etiquette *see* business etiquette
    layout 40
    protocol 81 *see also* business etiquette
optical disk 45
organisation and methods
    decision making 13
    delegation 13
    environmental responsibilities 13
    implementation of 12–13
    staff matters 13
organisational structure 3–4, 12
organising 6

P

pace-setting management 206
packaging 107
panel interview 144
paperless office 43
paper selection of applicants
    employment application form 139–140
    curriculum vitae 140–141
participating management 205
passive listening 72
peers 173, 175, 201
perception 101
performance evaluation
    methods of 171–173
    objectives 171
physiological needs 204
planning 6
policies 10, 12
Post Office Protocol (POP3) 51
pricing 108
privacy, right to *see* right to privacy
problem solving 70–71
product
    life cycle 109–110
    positioning 104
    promotions 109